CW01079765

The Top UK
AIR FRYER
COOKBOOK

150 Delicious, Affordable, and Easy Recipes the Whole Family Will Love

Hannah Holmes

ABOUT THE AUTHOR

We are simply a group of Chefs coming together to provide you the best Recipes we can, written with the metric system for a British audience & with ingredients easily found in all major UK Supermarkets!

We wanted to make our books the ultimate value for money so you get delicious recipes at a fair price, so we had to make the photos & coloured designs via the PDF accessible through the QR code.

There is a step by step guide on how to access your bonus PDF before the recipes page, please check there if you are confused.

You can access this on as many devices as you wish meaning you can take the document wherever you may be cooking!

We hope you enjoy!

And, if you have any questions please contact us via our email listed on the recipes and we will be happy to help & respond as fast as we can. Your happiness with our product is our main priority!We are simply a group of Chefs coming together to provide you the best Recipes we can, written with the metric system for a British audience & with ingredients easily found in all major UK Supermarkets!

We wanted to make our books the ultimate value for money so you get delicious recipes at a fair price, so we had to make the photos & coloured designs via the PDF accessible through the QR code.

There is a step by step guide on how to access your bonus PDF before the recipes page, please check there if you are confused.

You can access this on as many devices as you wish meaning you can take the document wherever you may be cooking!

We hope you enjoy!

And, if you have any questions please contact us via our email listed on the recipes and we will be happy to help & respond as fast as we can. Your happiness with our product is our main priority!

© **Copyright 2022 Hannah Holmes - All rights reserved.**

The content contained within this book may not be reproduced, duplicated or transmitted without direct written permission from the author or the publisher.

For permission requests, please contact the publisher at:

Under no circumstances will any blame or legal responsibility be held against the publisher, or author, for any damages, reparation, or monetary loss due to the information contained within this book. Either directly or indirectly.

Legal Notice:

This book is copyright protected. This book is only for personal use. You cannot amend, distribute, sell, use, quote or paraphrase any part, or the content within this book, without the consent of the author or publisher.

Disclaimer Notice:

Please note the information contained within this document is for educational and entertainment purposes only. All effort has been executed to present accurate, up to date, and reliable, complete information. No warranties of any kind are declared or implied. Readers acknowledge that the author is not engaging in the rendering of legal, financial, medical or professional advice.

The content within this book has been derived from various sources. By reading this document, the reader agrees that under no circumstances is the author responsible for any losses, direct or indirect, which are incurred as a result of the use of the information contained within this document, including, but not limited to: errors, omissions, or inaccuracies.

CONTENTS

INTRODUCTION

An air fryer is a popular kitchen appliance used to cook food. The air fryer works by circulating hot air around the food, which causes the food to cook evenly and quickly. Air fryers are available in a variety of sizes and styles, and they can be used to cook a wide range of foods. The most popular items to cook in an air fryer are chicken wings, French fries, and onion rings.

Air fryers are also becoming increasingly popular for cooking healthier versions of popular comfort foods, such as fried chicken or fish. Overall, air fryers are versatile and convenient kitchen appliances that can be used to cook a variety of foods.

If you are looking for a healthier way to fry your food, then an air fryer is a great option. Air fryers work by circulating hot air around the food, which allows them to cook quickly and evenly with little or no oil. This means that you can enjoy all your favourite fried foods without all the extra calories and fat. Plus, air fryers are very easy to use, so you'll be able to whip up delicious meals in no time. If you're looking for a healthier way to fry your food, then an air fryer is definitely the way to go.

Basics of an Air Fryer

An air fryer is a kitchen appliance that uses convection to cook food. The hot air circulates around the food, cooking it evenly on all sides. Air fryers come in a variety of sizes, but most have a basket that holds about 3–4kg of food. Here are 10 things you should know about air fryers:

1. Air fryers can be used to cook a variety of food, from chicken and steak to potatoes and veggies.

2. Most air fryers have a temperature range of 60–200 °C.

3. Air fryers work best when the food is cut into uniform pieces so that it cooks evenly.

4. Preheat the air fryer for about 3 minutes before adding the food to ensure optimal cooking results.

5. To avoid overcrowding the basket, cook food in batches if necessary.

6. Shake or flip the food midway through cooking to ensure even browning on all sides.

7. Use cooking spray or oil to help prevent sticking and promote even browning.

8. Always follow the manufacturer's instructions for safety and proper use.

9. Clean the air fryer basket after each use with soap and water or in the dishwasher.

10. Most air fryers have a warranty that covers defects in materials or workmanship; be sure to register your air fryer as soon as you purchase it to take advantage of this coverage.

Basics of Cooking in an Air Fryer

If you are new to using an air fryer, there are a few things you should know before getting started. Here are 10 basics of cooking in an air fryer:

1. **Preheat the air fryer.** Just like with a conventional oven, you'll need to preheat your air fryer before cooking. This will help ensure that your food cooks evenly.

2. **Add oil sparingly.** Because air fryers cook food by circulating hot air around it, adding too much oil will result in greasy, unhealthy food. Adding just a small amount of oil – or even better, spraying the cookware with a bit of cooking spray – will help ensure that your food doesn't stick and comes out crisp and golden brown.

3. **Shake the basket occasionally**. Air fryers work best when the food is in a single layer so that all pieces are exposed to the hot air. However, this also means that food can stick together and become soggy. To prevent this, shake the basket occasionally during cooking to redistribute the food and ensure even cooking.

4. **Do not overcrowd the basket.** Speaking of even cooking, it's important not to overcrowd the basket of your air fryer. If you overcrowd it, the hot air won't be able to circulate properly, and you'll end up with unevenly cooked food. So make sure to cook in batches if necessary.

5. **Cut food into uniform pieces.** Another way to ensure even cooking is to cut your food into uniform pieces before adding it to the air fryer. This way, all pieces will be exposed to the same amount of heat and will cook at the same rate.

6. **Know your cook times.** Air fryers can vary widely in terms of how long they take to cook food, so it is important to consult your air fryer's manual or a reliable recipe source to get accurate cook times. That way, you can avoid under- or overcooking your food.

7. **Use metal skewers cautiously.** If you are planning on using metal skewers in your air fryer (for example, for kebabs), be aware that they can conduct heat and cause uneven cooking if not used carefully. It is best to use metal skewers only if absolutely necessary, and if you do use them, be sure to preheat them along with the air fryer so that they don't shock the system when they're added later on.

8. **Be careful with frozen foods.** They can be tricky to cook in an air fryer because they often release ice crystals when heated, which can lead to uneven cooking. If you are planning on cooking frozen foods in your air fryer, it's best to consult a reliable recipe source for tips on how to do so successfully.

9. **Do not forget about safety.** Air fryers use hot oil or grease to cook food. There is always a risk of fire if they're used improperly. So be sure to read your air fryer's manual carefully before use, and never leave an air fryer unattended while it's in use. If you experience any problems during cooking, immediately unplug the appliance and contact the manufacturer for assistance.

10. **Do some experimentation.** Even if you follow all of these tips perfectly, there's still a chance that your first few attempts at using an air fryer might not go exactly as planned. That's why it's important to approach air frying with a sense of adventure and experiment until you find what works best for you and your appliance!

Why Air Fryers Are Becoming Popular

Air fryers have become a hot product in recent years, with sales skyrocketing as people learn more about their health benefits. Not only is air frying better for you than traditional deep frying, since there's no need to use oil, but it also results in food that has fewer calories and a crispier exterior.

Additionally, air fryers are an excellent timesaving device; they cook food quickly without the need to wait for a vat of oil to heat up or the need to manually flip food over while it fries. This convenience often makes meal prep much easier and more enjoyable. Moreover, because air fryers are available at varying prices and in different styles, there's something out there for everyone.

Features of an Air Fryer

With a new decade upon us, modern kitchen technologies like air fryers are becoming increasingly popular. Air fryers offer an innovative cooking solution that makes delicious food with less fat and calories than traditional deep-frying methods. Coming in many different sizes, models, and shapes to fit any need, these appliances are also convenient and come with a range of features.

From helpful timers to temperature sensors, air fryers provide users with many unique features that ensure healthy and superior cooking results. Whether you're looking for an easy way to whip up snacks or a full-course meal with greater efficiency and taste, air fryers can make it happen (with the right recipe and technique).

Air fryers are an incredible kitchen innovation that allow users to cook food with less oil, making it possible to quickly and easily produce healthier, delicious meals. Air fryers boast a variety of great features that make them extremely user-friendly. To begin with, air fryers are incredibly efficient when it comes to cooking time, allowing users to save up to 80% of their usual cooking time.

Additionally, air frying maintains the natural flavours and moisture of the food being cooked thanks to its hotter temperatures and turbo speed circulating hot air. Furthermore, many models are now equipped with features such as pre-programmed settings for popular dishes or automatic shutoffs for added safety.

As if all that wasn't enough, air fryers range in size from countertop-size models all the way down to personal, single-serve air fryers so everyone can find a perfect fit for their needs. The next time you're searching for an easy way to make healthier versions of your favourite recipes, be sure to consider an air fryer.

SPECS OF AN AIR FRYER

Technical Specs of an Air Fryer

Colour: Black and silver
Size: 3.7–5.8 quarts
Net Weight: 3.9kg
Material of Main Body: Plastic
Basket: 0.8kg
Basket Material: Alclad metal
Cord Length: 0.8m
Gross Weight: 5.2kg
Rated Voltage: 220–240V
Rated Frequency: 50–60Hz
Rated Power: 1425–1500W

General Specs of an Air Fryer

• Automatic shut-off
• Non-slip feet
• Cord storage
• Patented Rapid Air technology
• Ready signal
• Temperature control
• Time control
• Cool wall exterior

Cooking Times

When it comes to using an air fryer, there are a few things to keep in mind. First, preheat the air fryer according to the manufacturer's instructions. Second, cook in batches if possible so that the food has room to circulate and cook evenly. And finally, check on the food regularly to ensure that it is cooking properly. With those tips in mind, here are the cooking times for 10 popular air fryer dishes:

French fries: 20–30 minutes

Chicken wings: 20–25 minutes

Fish fillets: 10–15 minutes

Vegetable chips: 8–10 minutes

Chicken nuggets: 10–20 minutes

Mozzarella sticks: 6 minutes

Jalapeño poppers: 8 minutes

Pizza rolls 10 minutes

Cheesecake bites: 8 minutes

Keep in mind that these are just guidelines. Cooking times will vary depending on the size and thickness of your food. So be sure to keep an eye on your food as it cooks, and adjust the time accordingly. And don't forget to season your food before cooking! Seasoning will give your food even more flavour.

Best Way to Use an Air Fryer

Air fryers are one of the hottest appliances on the market, and it's no surprise why. They offer a healthier alternative to deep frying, and can be used to cook a variety of foods. If you're new to air frying, here are 10 tips to help you get the most out of your appliance:

1. Preheat the air fryer before cooking. This will help ensure that your food cooks evenly.

2. Cut food into even pieces. This will help ensure that all the food cooks evenly and prevents it from sticking together.

3. Use an oil sprayer to coat food lightly with oil. This helps to promote even browning and prevents sticking.

4. Do not overcrowd the basket. Air fryers work best when there is plenty of space around each piece of food. Otherwise, the food will steam instead of fry.

5. Shake the basket halfway through cooking. This helps redistribute the oil and prevents sticking.

6. Flip chicken or other meat halfway through cooking. This helps to ensure even cooking on both sides.

7. Broil foods for a crispier finish. Most air fryers have a built-in broil setting that can be used for a minute or two at the end of cooking to add a crispy finish to foods like chicken wings or fish fingers.

8. Use aluminium foil or a parchment paper liner in the basket for easy clean-up.

9. Be careful when opening the air fryer mid-cycle. The hot oil can cause burns.

10. Allow cooked food to rest for a few minutes before serving. This allows the juices to redistribute, preventing them from running out when you cut into the food.

Following these tips, you'll be well on your way to becoming an air frying pro!

How to Improve Taste and Crunchiness

Air frying is a popular cooking technique that uses hot air to cook food. While it can be used to cook a variety of foods, it is often used to make fried foods like chicken, fish, and French fries. One of the advantages of air frying is that it can improve the taste and crunchiness of these foods. Here are 5 tips to help you get the most out of your air fryer:

1. Preheat the air fryer before cooking. This will ensure that the food cooks evenly.

2. Use a light coat of oil on the food. This will create a crispy coating.

3. Cook the food in small batches. Overcrowding the air fryer can lead to soggy food.

4. Flip the food halfway through cooking. This will ensure even cooking.

5. Let the food cool slightly before serving. This will improve the crunchiness of the coating.

Following these tips, you should be able to produce delicious, crunchy air-fried foods that your whole family will enjoy!

Benefits of Using an Air Fryer

Air fryers are becoming increasingly popular for their convenience and health benefits. They offer a variety of advantages compared to traditional deep-frying. Air fryers use much less oil than traditional methods, resulting in overall lighter meals that are lower in fat and calories. The food cooked in an air fryer also retains more of its natural nutrients due to the shorter cooking times.

Additionally, air fryers produce a fraction of the smoke and odours that are produced when cooking with oil, making them ideal for those who do not want or cannot have their home filled with lingering frying smells. Furthermore, air fryers are also extremely easy to clean; since they do not require any oil to cook, most parts can be wiped down quickly and efficiently. Finally, as an added bonus, air fryers can cook multiple dishes simultaneously, helping you prepare your meals faster. With so many advantages to offer, it is no wonder why air fryers are becoming such a popular choice amongst at-home chefs!

Health Benefits

Air fryers offer a great way to enjoy fried foods without many of the unhealthy consequences. Recent studies have identified many health benefits associated with using an air fryer, including improved cardiac function, better digestion, lower risk of obesity, healthier fat intake, and higher levels of antioxidant compounds. These benefits are particularly evident when air frying vegetables like potatoes or leafy greens, which absorb fewer unhealthy oils than traditional deep-frying methods.

Air fryers also use significantly less energy and generate less waste than ovens, making them more ecologically friendly compared to other heating methods. They use hot air to quickly cook food evenly at a high temperature while dramatically reducing the amount of oil needed, resulting in healthier meals.

Air fryers are a great tool for those looking to maintain a healthy diet and lifestyle. Not only does it help with portion control, but other benefits include lower fat content in fried foods, improved nutrient retention, shorter cooking times for certain foods, heightened flavour due to less oil absorption, fewer calories consumed, and improved texture. Additionally, this type of method produces much less smoke and odour than traditional frying methods, making it a more appealing choice for home cooking.

All of these points combined make using an air fryer an incredibly smart choice for those who prioritise their health and well-being without compromising on taste. In short, air-fried dishes give you the same delicious results while simultaneously providing a range of enhanced health benefits!

Why Air Fryers Are a Healthy Option

Air fryers have become increasingly popular in recent years, and for good reason. Here are 4 ways that air fryers can benefit your health:

• Air fryers require less oil than traditional frying methods, which can reduce your intake of unhealthy fats.

• Air fryers cook food at a higher temperature than most other methods, which can kill harmful bacteria.

• Air fryers can preserve the nutrients in food, as opposed to methods like boiling or microwaving, which can cause nutrients to be lost in the cooking process.

• Air fryers can cook food evenly and prevent it from becoming overcooked or burnt, which can reduce the formation of harmful compounds.

Cleaning an Air Fryer

Cleaning an air fryer correctly and regularly is essential for its proper functioning, but it can be a difficult task – owing to the large number of parts and the intricate process for removing any built-up grease and debris. Thus, to help simplify things, here are some cleaning tips for air fryers:

1. Always clean the exterior of your unit with warm water and a nonabrasive solution; while it isn't eating up the grease or gunk cooking up inside, you still want to make sure it looks great!

2. After each use, wash all removable parts like racks, baskets, pans, and trays in warm soapy water or in a dishwasher.

3. Use a damp cloth to wipe off grime inside your machine; avoid abrasive materials when wiping down, as this could potentially damage your surfaces.

4. Remove any collected food residue on the underside of the tray by scrubbing with a brush; this should be done every few uses depending on cooking frequency.

5. After prepping all removable components in soapy water, allow them to soak for an adequate amount of time before rinsing. Ensure you use hot water and nonabrasive cleaning solutions for best results!

6. Dry components completely with a soft towel before inserting them back into your appliance.

7. Clean the fryer's air vent using either a softened bristle brush or a pipe cleaner.

8. If your unit came with instructions detailing how to deep clean it, be sure to follow those properly!

9. Consider changing out your filter bowl once every few weeks, unless you are using filtered tap water instead of plain tap water.

10. Look into buying some additional replacement parts such as heat shields and oil filters, if necessary, given the wear and tear over time; this will keep your appliance running smoothly while helping maintain its longevity.

FAQs

What Are the Benefits of Using an Air Fryer?

There are several benefits to using an air fryer. First, air fryers require less oil than traditional frying methods, which can result in healthier food. Second, air fryers cook food more evenly, which can lead to better flavour and texture. Third, air fryers can be used to cook a variety of foods, including meats, vegetables, and even desserts. Finally, air fryers are relatively easy to use and clean, making them a convenient option for busy cooks.

How Does an Air Fryer Work?

An air fryer works by circulating hot air around food to cook it evenly. The hot air is generated by an electric heating element, and the food is cooked in a basket or tray that is placed inside the fryer. This type of cooking is similar to convection cooking, and it allows food to be cooked quickly and evenly without the need for excessive amounts of oil.

How Do I Choose the Right Air Fryer?

When choosing an air fryer, there are several factors to consider. First, think about the size of the unit and the capacity you will need. Second, consider the features you would like your air fryer to have, such as a timer or adjustable temperature settings. Third, check reviews to see what other people have said about different models of air fryers. Finally, compare prices to find an air fryer that fits your budget.

What Are Some Tips for Using an Air Fryer?

Here are some tips for getting the most out of your air fryer:

- Preheat before adding food

- Cut food into uniform pieces so it cooks evenly

- Shake or flip foods halfway through cooking

- Add sauces or seasonings after cooking

- Clean the basket regularly to prevent sticking

Can I Use an Air Fryer if I Have Diabetes?

Yes! Air frying can be a great way to make healthier versions of your favourite fried foods. This cooking method requires less oil than traditional frying methods, which can reduce the number of unhealthy fats in your food. Additionally, air frying can preserve the nutrients in fruits and vegetables, making them a good option for people with diabetes who are looking for healthier ways to eat.

Breakfast Recipes

Hello! Please scan the QR code below to access your promised bonus of all our recipes with full colored photos & beautiful designs! It is the best we could do to keep the book as cheap as possible while providing the best value!

Also, once downloaded you can take the PDF with you digitally wherever you go- meaning you can cook these recipes wherever an Air Fryer is present!

STEP BY STEP Guide To Access-

1) Open Your Phones (Or Any Device You Want The Book On) Back Camera. The Back Camera Is The One You use as if you are taking a picture of someone.

2) Simply point your Camera at the QR code and 'tap' the QR code with your finger to focus the camera.

3) A link / pop up will appear. Simply tap that (and make sure you have internet connection) and the FREE PDF containing all of the colored images should appear.

4) If You Click On The File And It Says 'The File Is Too Big To Preview' Simply click 'Download' and it will download the full book onto your phone!

5) Now you have access to these FOREVER. Simply 'Bookmark' The tab it opened on, or download the document and take wherever you want.

6) Repeat this on any device you want it on!

Any Issues / Feedback / Troubleshooting please email: anthonypublishing123@gmail.com and our customer service team will help you! We want to make sure you have the BEST experience with our books!

French Toast

Prep. Time
10 minutes

Cook. Time
6 minutes

Yield
2 Servings

One of the best ways to prepare French toast for your breakfast table… This classic and tasty French toast is made with bread slices, eggs, evaporated milk, and sugar. You can prepare this French toast in an air fryer without the use of any extra oil or butter. Enjoy this French toast with the topping of maple syrup and fresh berries.

Energy value 109 Kcal | Protein 10.5g
Carbohydrates 1.4g | Fats 1.5g

Ingredients:

- Non-stick cooking spray
- 2 eggs
- 60ml evaporated milk
- 40g white sugar
- 10ml olive oil
- Dash of vanilla extract
- 4 wholewheat bread slices

Instructions:

Step 1: Grease the air fryer pan with cooking spray, then slide it inside.

Step 2: Adjust the temperature to 160 °C to preheat for 5 minutes and press the "Start/Pause" button to start preheating.

Step 3: In a large shallow bowl, add all the ingredients except for bread slices and whisk until well blended.

Step 4: Coat the bread slices with the egg mixture evenly.

Step 5: Place the bread slices into the preheated pan.

Step 6: Slide the pan inside and set the timer for 6 minutes.

Step 7: Press the "Start/Pause" button to start cooking.

Step 8: After 3 minutes of cooking, press the "Start/Pause" button to pause cooking and flip the bread slices.

Step 9: Again, press the "Start/Pause" button to resume cooking.

Step 10: After the cooking time has elapsed, remove the French toast from the air fryer and serve warm.

Savoury French Toast

Prep. Time
10 minutes

Cook. Time
4 minutes

Yield
2 Servings

The best-ever batch of savoury French toast… This deliciously savoury French toast is an easy-to-make option for breakfast. This savoury French toast is packed with scrumptiousness and vibrant flavours. This savoury French toast is great when served with yoghurt dip and fresh salad.

Energy value 227 Kcal | Protein 7.7g
Carbohydrates 41.4g | Fats 3.3g

Ingredients:

- 25g chickpea flour
- ¼ of green chilli, seeded and finely chopped
- 5g fresh coriander, finely chopped
- 25g onion, finely chopped
- 2.5g red chilli powder
- 1.25g ground cumin
- 1.25g ground turmeric
- Salt, as required
- Water, as required
- 4 wholewheat bread slices

Instructions:

Step 1: Add all the ingredients except bread slices in a large bowl and mix until a thick mixture forms.

Step 2: Spread the mixture over both sides of the bread slices.

Step 3: Line the air fryer pan with a piece of foil, then slide it inside.

Step 4: Adjust the temperature to 200 °C to preheat for 5 minutes and press "Start/Pause" button to start preheating.

Step 5: After preheating, place the bread slices in the prepared pan.

Step 6: Slide the pan in the air fryer and immediately set the temperature to 180 °C.

Step 7: Set the timer for 4 minutes and press the "Start/Pause" button to start cooking.

Step 8: After the cooking time has elapsed, remove the French toast from the air fryer and serve warm.

Cheesy Toast with Egg and Bacon

Prep. Time
15 minutes

Cook. Time
4 minutes

Yield
4 Servings

One of the easiest ways to prepare cheesy toast in an air fryer… You will love these lemony flavoured ricotta cheese-coated bread slices after being toasted to perfection in the air fryer. A serving of bacon and eggs makes a great combo with perfectly toasted bread slices.

Energy value 416 Kcal | Protein 27.2g
Carbohydrates 11.2g | Fats 29.3g

Ingredients:

- Non-stick cooking spray
- 4 white bread slices
- 115g ricotta cheese, crumbled
- Ground black pepper, as required
- 1 garlic clove, minced
- 1g lemon zest
- 4 cooked bacon slices
- 2 poached eggs

Instructions:

Step 1: In a food processor, add the garlic, ricotta, lemon zest, and black pepper. Pulse until smooth.

Step 2: Spread the ricotta mixture over each bread slice evenly.

Step 3: Grease the air fryer basket with cooking spray, then slide it inside.

Step 4: Adjust the temperature to 180 °C to preheat for 5 minutes and press the "Start/Pause" button to start preheating.

Step 5: After preheating, place the bread slices into the preheated air fryer basket.

Step 6: Slide the basket inside and set the timer for 4 minutes.

Step 7: Press the "Start/Pause" button to start cooking.

Step 8: After the cooking time has elapsed, remove the bread slices from the air fryer and transfer onto serving plates.

Step 9: Top with egg and bacon pieces and serve.

Bacon and Egg Cups

Prep. Time
10 minutes

Cook. Time
8 minutes

Yield
2 Servings

A very satisfying and flavoursome breakfast recipe without any fuss… These flavoursome bacon and egg cups come together so easily. This enchanting mix of bacon, eggs, milk, and marinara sauce makes a delicious breakfast. Garnishing of fresh parsley will add a delicious freshness.

Energy value 215 Kcal | Protein 14.9g
Carbohydrates 13.1g | Fats 11.4g

Ingredients:

- 1 cooked bacon slice, chopped
- 2 eggs
- 30ml whole milk
- Ground black pepper, as required
- 5g marinara sauce
- 10g Parmesan cheese, grated
- 2 bread slices, toasted and buttered

Instructions:

Step 1: Slide the air fryer basket inside and adjust the temperature to 180 °C to preheat for 5 minutes.

Step 2: Press the "Start/Pause" button to start preheating.

Step 3: Divide the bacon into 2 ramekins.

Step 4: Crack 1 egg into each ramekin over the bacon.

Step 5: Pour the milk over the eggs and sprinkle with black pepper.

Step 6: Top with marinara sauce, followed by the Parmesan cheese.

Step 7: After preheating, place the ramekins into the preheated air fryer basket.

Step 8: Slide the basket inside and set the timer for 8 minutes.

Step 9: Press the "Start/Pause" button to start cooking.

Step 10: After the cooking time has elapsed, remove the ramekins from the air fryer and serve hot alongside the bread slices.

Parsley and Jalapeño Soufflé

Prep. Time
10 minutes

Cook. Time
8 minutes

Yield
4 Servings

A comforting, yummy, and creamy recipe for breakfast… This savoury cream soufflé is a great option for a quick breakfast. The cream mingles with the parsley, jalapeño peppers, and eggs in a great way. Parsley and jalapeño soufflé is a delicious recipe for serving a crowd on busy mornings!

Energy value 82 Kcal | Protein 6.5g
Carbohydrates 1.3g | Fats 5.7g

Ingredients:

- Non-stick cooking spray
- 30ml single cream
- 3g fresh parsley, chopped
- Salt, as required
- 2 large eggs
- 1 jalapeño pepper, chopped

Instructions:

Step 1: Grease 2 ramekins with cooking spray.

Step 2: In a bowl, add all ingredients and beat until well combined.

Step 3: Divide the mixture into the prepared ramekins evenly.

Step 4: Slide the air fryer basket inside and adjust the temperature to 200 °C to preheat for 5 minutes.

Step 5: Press the "Start/Pause" button to start preheating.

Step 6: After preheating, place the ramekins into the preheated air fryer basket.

Step 7: Slide the basket inside and set the timer for 8 minutes.

Step 8: Press the "Start/Pause" button to start cooking.

Step 9: After the cooking time has elapsed, remove the ramekins from the air fryer and serve.

Cheese and Cream Omelette

Prep. Time
10 minutes

Cook. Time
8 minutes

Yield
2 Servings

A delicious and creamy textured omelette that is packed with eggs, cream, and cheddar cheese! Definitely a recipe to remember for those wanting a healthy and delicious breakfast… This air-fried omelette will satisfy you nicely. This omelette is great when served with buttered toast and ketchup.

Energy value 263 Kcal | Protein 15.8g
Carbohydrates 4.6g | Fats 20.4g

Ingredients:

- Non-stick cooking spray
- 4 eggs
- 60ml cream
- Salt and ground black pepper, as required
- 30g cheddar cheese

Instructions:

Step 1: Slide the air fryer basket inside and adjust the temperature to 175 °C to preheat for 5 minutes.

Step 2: Press the "Start/Pause" button to start preheating.

Step 3: Lightly grease a 6x3-inch baking dish with cooking spray.

Step 4: In a bowl, add the eggs, cream, salt, and black pepper, and beat until well combined.

Step 5: Place the egg mixture into the prepared baking dish.

Step 6: After preheating, place the baking dish into the preheated air fryer basket.

Step 7: Slide the basket inside and set the timer for 8 minutes.

Step 8: Press the "Start/Pause" button to start cooking.

Step 9: After 4 minutes of cooking, press the "Start/Pause" button to pause cooking and sprinkle the cheese on top of the omelette.

Step 10: Again, press the "Start/Pause" button to resume cooking.

Step 11: After the cooking time has elapsed, remove the baking dish from the air fryer and transfer the omelette onto a plate.

Step 12: Cut into 2 portions and serve hot.

Sausage and Bacon Omelette

 Prep. Time
10 minutes

 Cook. Time
10 minutes

 Yield
2 Servings

A rich and healthy air-fried omelette for breakfast… This omelette is loaded with the flavours of eggs, sausage, bacon, and onion. This omelette is a perfect choice if you want to eat some good food at your breakfast table. You can enjoy this meaty omelette with fresh herbs or a salsa dressing.

Energy value 500 Kcal | Protein 33.2g
Carbohydrates 6g | Fats 38.4g

Ingredients:

• Non-stick cooking spray
• 4 eggs
• 2 sausages, chopped
• 1 bacon slice, chopped
• 1 yellow onion, chopped

Instructions:

Step 1: Lightly grease a baking dish with cooking spray.

Step 2: In a bowl, whisk the eggs well.

Step 3: Add the remaining ingredients, and gently stir to combine.

Step 4: Place the mixture into the prepared baking dish.

Step 5: Slide the air fryer basket inside and adjust the temperature to 160 °C to preheat for 5 minutes.

Step 6: Press the "Start/Pause" button to start preheating.

Step 7: After preheating, place the baking dish into the preheated air fryer basket.

Step 8: Slide the basket inside and set the timer for 10 minutes.

Step 9: Press the "Start/Pause" button to start cooking.

Step 10: After the cooking time has elapsed, remove the baking dish from the air fryer and transfer the omelette onto a plate.

Step 11: Cut into equal-sized wedges and serve hot.

Courgette Omelette

 Prep. Time
15 minutes

 Cook. Time
14 minutes

 Yield
2 Servings

Definitely a keeper recipe for a healthy and delicious breakfast… A courgette omelette is a cheap, easy, but insanely delicious breakfast option for the whole family. This recipe will keep you energised all morning. Enjoy this veggie omelette alongside fresh cherry tomatoes and greens.

Energy value 159 Kcal | Protein 12.3g
Carbohydrates 4.1g | Fats 10.9g

Ingredients:

• Non-stick cooking spray
• 5g butter
• 1 courgette, julienned
• 4 eggs
• 5g fresh basil, chopped
• 1.25g red pepper flakes, crushed
• Salt and ground black pepper, as required

Instructions:

Step 1: Grease a baking dish with cooking spray.

Step 2: In a non-stick pan, melt butter over medium heat and cook the courgette for about 3–4 minutes.

Step 3: Remove the pan of courgette from the heat and set aside to cool slightly.

Step 4: Meanwhile, in a bowl, mix together the eggs, basil, red pepper flakes, salt, and black pepper.

Step 5: Add the cooked courgette, and gently stir to combine.

Step 6: Transfer the mixture into the prepared dish.

Step 7: Slide the air fryer basket inside and adjust the temperature to 180 °C to preheat for 5 minutes.

Step 8: Press the "Start/Pause" button to start preheating.

Step 9: After preheating, place the baking dish into the preheated air fryer basket.

Step 10: Slide the basket inside and set the timer for 10 minutes.

Step 11: Press the "Start/Pause" button to start cooking.

Step 12: After the cooking time has elapsed, remove the baking dish from the air fryer and transfer the omelette onto a plate.

Step 13: Cut into equal-sized wedges and serve hot. cooking.

Chicken and Broccoli Quiche

Prep. Time
15 minutes

Cook. Time
12 minutes

Yield
6 Servings

One of the most delicious and healthy recipes for breakfast… When the morning hunger strikes you, there is nothing better to satisfy it than this scrumptious breakfast quiche. This tasty and nutrient-dense quiche is a perfect start to your day. Fresh green salad is a great accompaniment to this dish.

Energy value 234 Kcal | Protein 6g
Carbohydrates 22.4g | Fats 13.8g

Ingredients:

- Non-stick cooking spray
- 1 frozen ready-made pie crust
- 1 egg
- 40g cheddar cheese, grated
- 45ml whipping cream
- Salt and freshly ground black pepper, to taste
- 25g boiled broccoli, chopped
- 35g cooked chicken, chopped

Instructions:

Step 1: Lightly grease 2 small pie pans with cooking spray.

Step 2: Cut 2x5-inch circles from the pie crust.

Step 3: Place a pie crust circle in each pie pan, and gently press in the bottom and sides.

Step 4: In a bowl, mix together the egg, cheese, cream, salt, and black pepper.

Step 5: Pour the egg mixture over the dough base and top with the broccoli and chicken.

Step 6: Slide the air fryer basket inside and adjust the temperature to 200 ºC to preheat for 5 minutes.

Step 7: Press the "Start/Pause" button to start preheating.

Step 8: After preheating, place the pie pans into the preheated air fryer basket.

Step 9: Slide the basket inside and set the timer for 12 minutes.

Step 10: Press the "Start/Pause" button to start cooking.

Step 11: After the cooking time has elapsed, remove the pie pans from the air fryer and place onto a wire rack to cool for about 5 minutes before serving.

Step 12: Cut into equal-sized wedges and serve hot.

Salmon Quiche

Prep. Time
15 minutes

Cook. Time
20 minutes

Yield
2 Servings

A great twist on a breakfast quiche! A super-easy and delicious recipe of scrumptious quiche for breakfast… The combo of salmon, eggs, butter, and heavy cream adds extra flavour to the quiche. This salmon quiche recipe is worthy of an Easter dinner for the whole family!

Energy value 596 Kcal | Protein 27.2g
Carbohydrates 34.4g | Fats 39.1g

Ingredients:

- 155g salmon fillet, chopped
- 10ml fresh lemon juice
- Salt and ground black pepper, as required
- 1 egg yolk
- 50g chilled butter
- 85g plain flour
- 20ml cold water
- 2 eggs
- 45ml whipping cream
- 1 green onion, chopped

Instructions:

Step 1: In a bowl, mix together the salmon, salt, black pepper, and lemon juice. Set aside.

Step 2: In another bowl, add egg yolk, butter, flour, and water. Mix until a dough forms. Place the dough onto a floured smooth surface and roll into a circle of about 7 inch.

Step 3: Place the dough into a quiche pan and press firmly in the bottom and along the edges. Trim the excess edges.

Step 4: In a small bowl, add the eggs, cream, salt, and black pepper, and beat until well combined.

Step 5: Place the cream mixture over the crust evenly, and top with the chopped salmon, followed by the green onion.

Step 6: Slide the air fryer basket inside and adjust the temperature to 180 ºC to preheat for 5 minutes. Press the "Start/Pause" button to start preheating.

Step 7: After preheating, place the quiche pan into the preheated air fryer basket.

Step 8: Slide the basket inside and set the timer for 20 minutes. Press the "Start/Pause" button to start cooking.

Step 9: After the cooking time has elapsed, remove the quiche pan from the air fryer and place onto a wire rack to cool for about 5 minutes before serving.

Step 10: Cut into equal-sized wedges and serve hot.

Veggie Frittata

Prep. Time
15 minutes

Cook. Time
18 minutes

Yield
2 Servings

Garden-fresh spinach, tomato, onion, feta cheese, half-and-half, and eggs team up greatly for this breakfast frittata. This tasty and simple veggie frittata recipe will be well received at your breakfast table. The whole family will enjoy this veggie-packed frittata. Enjoy with a bowl of fresh fruit.

Energy value 278 Kcal | Protein 18.8g
Carbohydrates 8g | Fats 19.4g

Ingredients:

- 60ml half-and-half
- 4 large eggs
- Salt and ground black pepper, as required
- 60g fresh spinach, chopped
- 60g onion, chopped
- 50g tomato, chopped
- 55g feta cheese, crumbled

Instructions:

Step 1: In a bowl, add the half-and-half, eggs, salt, and black pepper. Beat until well combined.

Step 2: Add the spinach, onion, tomatoes, and feta cheese, and mix well.

Step 3: Place the mixture into a baking dish.

Step 4: Slide the air fryer basket inside and adjust the temperature to 185 °C to preheat for 5 minutes.

Step 5: Press the "Start/Pause" button to start preheating.

Step 6: After preheating, place the baking dish into the preheated air fryer basket.

Step 7: Slide the basket inside and set the timer for 18 minutes.

Step 8: Press the "Start/Pause" button to start cooking.

Step 9: After the cooking time has elapsed, remove the baking dish from the air fryer and place onto a wire rack to cool for about 5 minutes before serving.

Step 10: Cut into equal-sized wedges and serve hot.

Sausage and Bell Pepper Casserole

Prep. Time
15 minutes

Cook. Time
25 minutes

Yield
6 Servings

A breakfast casserole that surely everyone will love… This decadent and tasty casserole is a great treat for the holiday breakfast table. Sausage, eggs, cheddar cheese, bell pepper, and seasonings all feature in this casserole. Enjoy with toasted buttery English muffins.

Energy value 391 Kcal | Protein 24.4g
Carbohydrates 2.5g | Fats 31.1g

Ingredients:

- 5ml olive oil
- 455g ground sausage
- 1 bell pepper, seeded and chopped
- 30g onion, chopped
- 55g cheddar cheese, grated
- 2.5g garlic salt
- 5g fennel seeds
- 8 eggs, beaten

Instructions:

Step 1: In a skillet, heat the oil over medium heat and cook the sausage for about 4–5 minutes.

Step 2: Add the bell pepper and onion, and cook for about 4–5 minutes.

Step 3: Remove from the heat and transfer the sausage mixture into a bowl to cool slightly.

Step 4: Place the sausage mixture in a baking dish and top with the cheese, followed by the beaten eggs, fennel seed, and garlic salt.

Step 5: Slide the air fryer basket inside and adjust the temperature to 200 °C to preheat for 5 minutes.

Step 6: Press the "Start/Pause" button to start preheating.

Step 7: After preheating, place the baking dish into the preheated air fryer basket.

Step 8: Slide the basket inside and set the timer for 15 minutes.

Step 9: Press the "Start/Pause" button to start cooking.

Step 10: After the cooking time has elapsed, remove the baking dish from the air fryer and set the timer for 15 minutes.

Step 11: Cut into equal-sized wedges and serve hot.

Potato Rosti

Prep. Time
15 minutes

Cook. Time
15 minutes

Yield
2 Servings

One of the best potato rosti recipes that is deliciously silky and tender on the inside and crispy on the outside. This delicious potato rosti is perfect for lazy weekend breakfasts. This delicious and crispy potato rosti is made with grated potatoes, fresh chives, and seasoning. This potato rosti can be enjoyed with a topping of sour cream.

Energy value 99 Kcal | Protein 2g
Carbohydrates 17.8g | Fats 2.5g

Ingredients:

- 5ml olive oil
- 225g Yukon gold potatoes, peeled and roughly grated
- 5g fresh chives, finely chopped
- Salt and ground black pepper, as required

Instructions:

Step 1: Grease a pizza pan with olive oil.

Step 2: In a large bowl, mix together the potatoes, chives, salt, and black pepper.

Step 3: Place the potato mixture into the prepared pizza pan.

Step 4: Slide the air fryer basket inside and adjust the temperature to 180 °C to preheat for 5 minutes.

Step 5: Press the "Start/Pause" button to start preheating.

Step 6: After preheating, place the pizza pan into the preheated air fryer basket.

Step 7: Slide the basket inside and set the timer for 15 minutes.

Step 8: Press the "Start/Pause" button to start cooking.

Step 9: After the cooking time has elapsed, remove the pizza pan from the air fryer and set aside for about 5 minutes.

Step 10: Cut the potato rosti into wedges and serve.

Courgette Fritters

Prep. Time
15 minutes

Cook. Time
7 minutes

Yield
4 Servings

A crowd-pleasing recipe of fritters that are fluffy on the inside and lightly crispy on the outside… These fritters are delicately flavoured with courgette, halloumi cheese, dill, and eggs. This fritter recipe is a must-try if you are a true fan of the summer staple courgette. Tzatziki sauce accompanies these fritters nicely.

Energy value 259 Kcal | Protein 15.5g
Carbohydrates 10.9g | Fats 7.4g

Ingredients:

- Non-stick cooking spray
- 300g courgette, grated and squeezed
- 200g halloumi cheese
- 35g plain flour
- 2 eggs
- 2g fresh dill, minced
- Salt and ground black pepper, as required

Instructions:

Step 1: In a large bowl, add all the ingredients and mix well.

Step 2: Make small-sized fritters from the mixture.

Step 3: Grease a baking dish with cooking spray.

Step 4: Place the fritters into the prepared baking dish.

Step 5: Slide the air fryer basket inside and adjust the temperature to 180 °C to preheat for 5 minutes.

Step 6: Press the "Start/Pause" button to start preheating.

Step 7: After preheating, place the baking dish into the preheated air fryer basket.

Step 8: Slide the basket inside and set the timer for 6–7 minutes.

Step 9: Press the "Start/Pause" button to start cooking.

Step 10: After the cooking time has elapsed, remove the baking dish from the air fryer and serve warm.

Oat and Raisin Muffins

Prep. Time
15 minutes

Cook. Time
10 minutes

Yield
4 Servings

A great breakfast with a combination of oats, butter, raisins, and eggs… Surely these muffins will be a hit, even for the pickiest eater. These decadent and delicious oat muffins are a perfect blend of sweetness, crunch, and moistness. These muffins are perfectly baked in the air fryer.

Energy value 409 Kcal | Protein 5.8g
Carbohydrates 40.6g | Fats 25.7g

Ingredients:

- Non-stick cooking spray
- Non-stick cooking spray
- 65g plain flour
- 25g rolled oats
- 0.5g baking powder
- 65g icing sugar
- 115g butter, softened
- 2 eggs
- 1.25ml vanilla extract
- 40g raisins

Instructions:

Step 1: Grease 4 muffin moulds with cooking spray.

Step 2: In a bowl, mix together the flour, oats, and baking powder.

Step 3: In another bowl, add the sugar and butter, and beat until creamy texture is formed.

Step 4: Then add in the egg and vanilla extract, and beat until well combined. Add the egg mixture into the oat mixture and mix until just combined.

Step 5: Fold in the raisins.

Step 6: Slide the air fryer basket inside and adjust the temperature to 180 °C to preheat for 5 minutes. Press the "Start/Pause" button to start preheating.

Step 7: After preheating, place the muffin moulds into the preheated air fryer basket.

Step 8: Slide the basket inside and set the timer for 10 minutes. Press the "Start/Pause" button to start cooking.

Step 9: After the cooking time has elapsed, remove the muffin moulds from the air fryer and place onto a wire rack to cool for about 10 minutes.

Step 10: Then invert the muffins on the wire rack to completely cool before serving.

Apple Muffins

Prep. Time
15 minutes

Cook. Time
25 minutes

Yield
12 Servings

Looking for something healthy and nutritious for breakfast? Here is a perfect recipe just for you: apple muffins! These muffins are packed with the flavours of healthy apple, milk, applesauce, and deliciously warm spices. Surely this recipe will join your muffin club permanently.

Energy value 110 Kcal | Protein 2.1g
Carbohydrates 25.3g | Fats 0.2g

Ingredients:

- Non-stick cooking spray
- 115g plain flour
- 40g sugar
- 3g baking powder
- 1.25g ground cinnamon
- 1g ground ginger
- 1g salt
- 180ml milk
- 50g applesauce
- 60g apple, cored and chopped

Instructions:

Step 1: Grease 6 muffin moulds with cooking spray.

Step 2: In a large bowl, mix together the flour, sugar, baking powder, spices, and salt.

Step 3: Add in the milk and applesauce, and beat until just combined.

Step 4: Fold in the chopped apple.

Step 5: Place the mixture into the prepared muffin moulds evenly.

Step 6: Slide the air fryer basket inside and adjust the temperature to 200 °C to preheat for 5 minutes.

Step 7: Press the "Start/Pause" button to start preheating.

Step 8: After preheating, place the muffin moulds into the preheated air fryer basket.

Step 9: Slide the basket inside and set the timer for 25 minutes. Press the "Start/Pause" button to start cooking.

Step 10: After the cooking time has elapsed, remove the muffin moulds from the air fryer and place onto a wire rack to cool for about 10 minutes.

Step 11: Then invert the muffins on the wire rack to completely cool before serving.

Banana Muffins

Prep. Time
10 minutes

Cook. Time
10 minutes

Yield
4 Servings

One of the best recipes for a healthy weekday breakfast... Here is a bakery-style recipe of muffins with an amazingly tasty flavour and a wonderful aroma! These fluffy and sweet muffins are packed with nutritious and delicious flavours of sweet banana, crunchy walnut, and best-quality butter.

Energy value 229 Kcal | Protein 3g
Carbohydrates 24.6g | Fats 14g

Ingredients:

- Non-stick cooking spray
- 25g oats
- 35g refined flour
- 2g baking powder
- 35g icing sugar
- 55g unsalted butter, softened
- 5ml whole milk
- 75g banana, peeled and mashed
- 1.25g vanilla extract
- 15g walnuts, chopped

Instructions:

Step 1: Grease 4 muffin moulds with cooking spray.

Step 2: In a bowl, mix together the oats, flour, and baking powder.

Step 3: In another bowl, add the sugar and butter, and beat until creamy. Add the banana and vanilla extract, and beat until well combined.

Step 4: Add the flour mixture and milk into the banana mixture, and mix until just combined.

Step 5: Fold in the walnuts.Place the mixture into the prepared muffin moulds evenly.

Step 6: Slide the air fryer basket inside and adjust the temperature to 160 ºC to preheat for 5 minutes. Press the "Start/Pause" button to start preheating.

Step 7: After preheating, place the muffin moulds into the preheated air fryer basket. Slide the basket inside and set the timer for 10 minutes. Press the "Start/Pause" button to start cooking.

Step 8: After the cooking time has elapsed, remove the moulds from the air fryer and place onto a wire rack to cool for about 10 minutes.

Step 9: Invert the muffins on the wire rack to cool completely before serving.

Banana Bread

Prep. Time
10 minutes

Cook. Time
20 minutes

Yield
8 Servings

An absolutely delicious and classic breakfast bread recipe that is incredibly moist with loads of banana flavour.... This recipe makes nutritiously healthy bread that boasts banana flavour in a delicious way. Your whole house is sure to be filled with the warmth and deliciousness of this banana bread.

Energy value 301 Kcal | Protein 3.6g
Carbohydrates 41.1g | Fats 14.9g

Ingredients:

- Non-stick cooking spray
- 200g plain flour
- 85g sugar
- 4g baking powder
- 4g baking soda
- 5g ground cinnamon
- 5g salt
- 3 bananas, peeled and sliced
- 120ml whole milk
- 120ml olive oil

Instructions:

Step 1: Grease a loaf pan with cooking spray.

Step 2: In the bowl of a stand mixer, add all the ingredients and mix well.

Step 3: Place the mixture into the prepared loaf pan.

Step 4: Slide the air fryer basket inside and adjust the temperature to 165 ºC to preheat for 5 minutes.

Step 5: Press the "Start/Pause" button to start preheating.

Step 6: After preheating, place the loaf pan into the preheated air fryer basket.

Step 7: Slide the basket inside and set the timer for 20 minutes.

Step 8: Press the "Start/Pause" button to start cooking.

Step 9: After the cooking time has elapsed, remove the loaf pan from the air fryer and place onto a wire rack for about 10–15 minutes.

Step 10: Invert the bread on the wire rack to cool completely before slicing.

Step 11: Cut the bread into slices of the desired size and serve.

Courgette Bread

Prep. Time
15 minutes

Cook. Time
20 minutes

Yield
8 Servings

Do you want to try a wonderful wheat bread with courgette that's in season? Try this classic courgette bread recipe that is moist and delicious… It's deliciously flavoured with garden-fresh courgette, warm cinnamon, aromatic vanilla extract, and crunchy walnuts in every bite.

Energy value 367 Kcal I Protein 5.2g
Carbohydrates 47.4g I Fats 18.6g

Ingredients:

- Non-stick cooking spray
- 180g plain flour, plus more for dusting
- 2g baking powder
- 2g baking soda
- 5g ground cinnamon
- 2g salt
- 225g sugar
- 120ml vegetable oil
- 2 small eggs
- 5ml vanilla extract
- 175g courgette, grated
- 50g walnuts, chopped

Instructions:

Step 1: Grease 1 (8x4-inch) loaf pan with cooking spray, then dust lightly with flour.

Step 2: In a bowl, mix together the flour, baking powder, baking soda, cinnamon, and salt.

Step 3: In another large bowl, add the sugar, oil, eggs, and vanilla extract, and beat until well combined.

Step 4: Then add in the flour mixture and stir until just combined.

Step 5: Gently fold in the courgette and walnuts. Place the mixture into the prepared loaf pan evenly.

Step 6: Slide the air fryer basket inside and adjust the temperature to 160 °C to preheat for 5 minutes. Press the "Start/Pause" button to start preheating.

Step 7: After preheating, place the loaf pan into the preheated air fryer basket. Slide the basket inside and set the timer for 20 minutes. Press the "Start/Pause" button to start cooking.

Step 8: After the cooking time has elapsed, remove the loaf pan from the air fryer and place onto a wire rack for about 10–15 minutes.

Step 9: Then remove the bread from the pan and place onto the wire rack to cool completely before slicing.

Eggs in Avocado Cups

Prep. Time
10 minutes

Cook. Time
22 minutes

Yield
2 Servings

Here is a recipe for scrumptiously baked eggs in avocado cups that you can prepare in an air fryer easily. This simple yet satisfying breakfast is a wonderful treat for egg lovers. Protein-packed eggs make a wonderful combo with avocados (which are great for heart health). You can enjoy this breakfast treat with a topping of crispy bacon pieces.

Energy value 292 Kcal I Protein 9.9g
Carbohydrates 9.3g I Fats 25.6g

Ingredients:

- 1 large ripe avocado, halved and pitted
- 2 eggs
- Salt and ground black pepper, as required
- Non-stick cooking spray
- 15g Parmesan cheese, grated
- 2g fresh chives, minced

Instructions:

Step 1: With a spoon, scoop out some of the flesh from the avocado halves to make a hole.

Step 2: Crack 1 egg into each avocado half and sprinkle with salt and black pepper.

Step 3: Grease the air fryer basket with cooking spray, then slide it inside.

Step 4: Adjust the temperature of the air fryer to 175 °C to preheat for 5 minutes and press the "Start/Pause" button to start preheating.

Step 5: After preheating, place the avocado halves into the preheated air fryer basket.

Step 6: Slide the basket inside and set the timer for 22 minutes.

Step 7: Press the "Start/Pause" button to start cooking.

Step 8: After 12 minutes of cooking, press the "Start/Pause" button to pause cooking.

Step 9: Sprinkle the top of the avocado halves with Parmesan cheese, then press the "Start/Pause" button to resume cooking.

Step 10: After the cooking time has elapsed, remove the avocado halves from the air fryer.

Step 11: Serve hot with a garnishing of chives.

Poultry Recipes

Hello! Please scan the QR code below to access your promised bonus of all our recipes with full colored photos & beautiful designs! It is the best we could do to keep the book as cheap as possible while providing the best value!

Also, once downloaded you can take the PDF with you digitally wherever you go- meaning you can cook these recipes wherever an Air Fryer is present!

STEP BY STEP Guide To Access-

1) Open Your Phones (Or Any Device You Want The Book On) Back Camera. The Back Camera Is The One You use as if you are taking a picture of someone.

2) Simply point your Camera at the QR code and 'tap' the QR code with your finger to focus the camera.

3) A link / pop up will appear. Simply tap that (and make sure you have internet connection) and the FREE PDF containing all of the colored images should appear.

4) If You Click On The File And It Says 'The File Is Too Big To Preview' Simply click 'Download' and it will download the full book onto your phone!

5) Now you have access to these FOREVER. Simply 'Bookmark' The tab it opened on, or download the document and take wherever you want.

6) Repeat this on any device you want it on!

Any Issues / Feedback / Troubleshooting please email: anthonypublishing123@gmail.com and our customer service team will help you! We want to make sure you have the BEST experience with our books!

Herbed Cornish Game Hen

Prep. Time
15 minutes

Cook. Time
16 minutes

Yield
4 Servings

If you want an elegant dinner that is simple to make, then your search ends with this classic recipe. Try this truly delicious recipe of Cornish game hen for a special occasion! This hen is cooked in an air fryer to crispy perfection. A combo of fresh herbs, lemon zest, and seasoning brings out the refreshing flavours of this roasted hen.

Energy value 698 Kcal | Protein 38.7g
Carbohydrates 2g | Fats 61.1g

Ingredients:

- 120ml olive oil
- 1.5g fresh rosemary, chopped
- 1.5g fresh thyme, chopped
- 1.5g fresh lemon zest, grated
- 5g sugar
- 1.25g red pepper flakes, crushed
- Salt and ground black pepper, as required
- 910g Cornish game hen, backbone removed and halved
- Non-stick cooking spray

Instructions:

Step 1: In a bowl, mix together the oil, herbs, lemon zest, sugar, and spices.

Step 2: Add the hen portions and generously coat with the marinade.

Step 3: Cover and refrigerate for about 24 hours.

Step 4: In a strainer, place the hen portions and set aside to drain any liquid.

Step 5: Grease the air fryer basket with cooking spray, then slide it inside.

Step 6: Adjust the temperature to 200 °C to preheat for 5 minutes and press the "Start/Pause" button to start preheating.

Step 7: After preheating, place the hen portions into the preheated air fryer basket.

Step 8: Slide the basket inside and set the timer for 14–16 minutes.

Step 9: Press the "Start/Pause" button to start cooking.

Step 10: After the cooking time has elapsed, remove the hen portions from the air fryer and serve.

Serving Suggestion: Serve this Cornish game hen with buttered potatoes.

Simple Whole Chicken

Prep. Time
15 minutes

Cook. Time
40 minutes

Yield
2 Servings

A wonderful weeknight meal with a touch of elegance… A simple roasted whole chicken that is delicious and full of healthy protein. This simple salt-and-black-pepper-seasoned whole chicken is perfectly cooked in the air fryer with all its natural juices. This simple yet elegant roasted chicken will bring the wow factor to your dinner party.

Energy value 698 Kcal | Protein 63.8g
Carbohydrates 0g | Fats 49.6g

Ingredients:

- Non-stick cooking spray
- 1 whole chicken (680g)
- Salt and ground black pepper, as required
- 15ml olive oil

Instructions:

Step 1: Grease the air fryer basket with cooking spray, then slide it inside.

Step 2: Adjust the temperature to 200 °C to preheat for 5 minutes and press the "Start/Pause" button to start preheating.

Step 3: Season the chicken with salt and black pepper, then coat with oil evenly.

Step 4: After preheating, place the chicken into the preheated air fryer basket.

Step 5: Slide the basket inside and set the timer for 35–40 minutes.

Step 6: Press the "Start/Pause" button to start cooking.

Step 7: After the cooking time has elapsed, remove the chicken from the air fryer and place onto a platter for about 10–15 minutes before serving.

Step 8: Cut the chicken into pieces of the desired size and serve.

Serving Suggestion: Serve chicken with gravy.

Spiced Whole Chicken

Prep. Time
10 minutes

Cook. Time
1 hour

Yield
6 Servings

A whole chicken is one of the easiest things to cook in an air fryer! Try this heavenly roasted chicken recipe with a delicious spicy flair… This air fryer recipe delivers a roasted chicken with crispy skin and juicy meat. The combo of spices and olive oil adds a delicious taste to the roasted chicken.

Energy value 781 Kcal | Protein 67.7g
Carbohydrates 3.5g | Fats 54.4g

Ingredients:

- Non-stick cooking spray
- 5g dried thyme
- 10g paprika
- 5g cayenne powder
- 5g onion powder
- 5g garlic powder
- 5g ground white pepper
- Salt and ground black pepper, as required
- 1 whole chicken (2.25kg), neck and giblets removed
- 45ml olive oil

Instructions:

Step 1: In a bowl, mix together the thyme, spices, salt, and black pepper.

Step 2: Coat the chicken with 30ml of oil, then rub inside, outside, and underneath the skin with half of the herb mixture generously.

Step 3: Grease the air fryer basket with cooking spray, then slide it inside. Adjust the temperature of the air fryer to 175 °C to preheat for 5 minutes and press the "Start/Pause" button to start preheating.

Step 4: After preheating, place the chicken into the preheated air fryer basket, breast-side down. Slide the basket inside and set the timer for 60 minutes. Press the "Start/Pause" button to start cooking. After 30 minutes of cooking, press the "Start/Pause" button to pause cooking.

Step 5: Flip the chicken and coat with the remaining oil. Then rub the chicken with the remaining herb mixture. Again, press the "Start/Pause" button to resume cooking.

Step 6: After the cooking time has elapsed, remove the chicken from the air fryer and place onto a platter for about 10 minutes before carving.

Step 7: Cut the chicken into pieces of the desired size and serve.

Serving Suggestion: Serve chicken with steamed green beans.

Spicy Chicken Legs

Prep. Time
15 minutes

Cook. Time
20 minutes

Yield
4 Servings

Do you want a plate of perfectly cooked chicken legs at your dining table? Then try this recipe of moist and luscious chicken legs with a great combination of spices… The wonderful blend of ginger, garlic, Greek yoghurt, and spices adds a delicious flavour.

Energy value 507 Kcal | Protein 19.6g
Carbohydrates 2.8g | Fats 18.9g

Ingredients:

- 4 chicken legs
- 45ml fresh lemon juice
- 2g fresh ginger, minced
- 2g garlic, minced
- Salt, as required
- 60g plain Greek yoghurt
- 10g red chilli powder
- 5g ground cumin
- Ground black pepper, as required

Instructions:

Step 1: In a bowl, mix together the chicken legs, lemon juice, ginger, garlic, and salt. Set aside for about 15 minutes.

Step 2: Meanwhile, in another large bowl, mix together the yoghurt and spices.

Step 3: Add the chicken legs and coat with the spice mixture generously.

Step 4: Cover the bowl and refrigerate for at least 10–12 hours.

Step 5: Line the air fryer basket with a piece of foil, then slide it inside.

Step 6: Adjust the temperature to 230 °C to preheat for 5 minutes and press the "Start/Pause" button to start preheating.

Step 7: After preheating, place the chicken legs into the preheated air fryer basket.

Step 8: Slide the basket inside and set the timer for 18–20 minutes.

Step 9: Press the "Start/Pause" button to start cooking.

Step 10: After the cooking time has elapsed, remove the chicken legs from the air fryer and serve hot.

Serving Suggestion: Serve chicken legs with buttery mashed potato.

Glazed Chicken Drumsticks

Prep. Time
10 minutes

Cook. Time
22 minutes

Yield
4 Servings

Sweet and sticky chicken drumsticks with a wonderfully delicious taste... This great marinade of Dijon mustard, honey, oil, fresh herbs, and seasoning deeply accentuates the deliciousness of the drumsticks. These sticky glazed chicken drumsticks are finger-licking delicious.

Energy value 292 Kcal | Protein 25.1g
Carbohydrates 5.8g | Fats 18.6g

Ingredients:

- Non-stick cooking spray
- 80g Dijon mustard
- 15g honey
- 30ml olive oil
- 2g fresh thyme, minced
- 1g fresh rosemary, minced
- Salt and ground black pepper, as required
- 4x150g boneless chicken drumsticks

Instructions:

Step 1: In a bowl, add the mustard, honey, oil, herbs, salt, and black pepper, and mix well.

Step 2: Add the drumsticks and coat with the mixture generously.

Step 3: Cover and refrigerate to marinate overnight.

Step 4: Grease the air fryer basket with cooking spray, then slide it inside.

Step 5: Adjust the temperature to 160 °C to preheat for 5 minutes and press the "Start/Pause" button to start preheating.

Step 6: After preheating, place the chicken drumsticks into the preheated air fryer basket.

Step 7: Slide the basket inside and set the timer for 12 minutes.

Step 8: Press the "Start/Pause" button to start cooking.

Step 9: After 12 minutes of cooking, set the temperature of the air fryer to 180 °C for 10 more minutes.

Step 10: After the cooking time has elapsed, remove the chicken drumsticks from the air fryer and serve hot.

Serving Suggestion: Serve these chicken drumsticks with fresh green salad.

Gingered Chicken Drumsticks

Prep. Time
15 minutes

Cook. Time
25 minutes

Yield
3 Servings

A magnificent roasted chicken drumsticks recipe... Use a magnificent combo of coconut milk, ginger, galangal, turmeric, and paprika, and you are on your way to having delicious air-fried chicken drumsticks. Surely your whole family will be impressed by this recipe of chicken drumsticks.

Energy value 344 Kcal | Protein 47.5g
Carbohydrates 3.8g | Fats 14.2g

Ingredients:

- 60ml full-fat coconut milk
- 3.5g fresh ginger, minced
- 3.5g fresh galangal, minced
- 5g ground turmeric
- 5g paprika
- Salt and ground black pepper, as required
- 3x170g chicken drumsticks
- Non-stick cooking spray

Instructions:

Step 1: In a bowl, mix together the coconut milk, galangal, ginger, and spices.

Step 2: Add the chicken drumsticks and generously coat with the marinade.

Step 3: Refrigerate to marinate for at least 6–8 hours.

Step 4: Grease the air fryer basket with cooking spray, then slide it inside.

Step 5: Adjust the temperature to 190 °C to preheat for 5 minutes and press the "Start/Pause" button to start preheating.

Step 6: After preheating, place the chicken drumsticks into the preheated air fryer basket.

Step 7: Slide the basket inside and set the timer for 20–25 minutes.

Step 8: Press the "Start/Pause" button to start cooking.

Step 9: After the cooking time has elapsed, remove the chicken drumsticks from the air fryer and serve hot.

Serving Suggestion: Serve these chicken drumsticks with garlicky broccoli.

Lemony Chicken Thighs

Prep. Time
10 minutes

Cook. Time
20 minutes

Yield
6 Servings

A magnificent roasted chicken drumsticks recipe... Use a magnificent combo of coconut milk, ginger, galangal, turmeric, and paprika, and you are on your way to having delicious air-fried chicken drumsticks. Surely your whole family will be impressed by this recipe of chicken drumsticks.

Energy value 367 Kcal | Protein 49.3g
Carbohydrates 0.4g | Fats 17.5g

Ingredients:

- Non-stick cooking spray
- 6x170g chicken thighs
- 30ml fresh lemon juice
- 30ml olive oil
- 3g Italian seasoning
- Salt and ground black pepper, as required
- 1 lemon, sliced thinly

Instructions:

Step 1: In a large bowl, add all the ingredients except for lemon slices. Toss to coat well.

Step 2: Refrigerate to marinate for 30 minutes to overnight.

Step 3: Remove the chicken thighs from the bowl and let any excess marinade drip off.

Step 4: Grease the air fryer basket with cooking spray, then slide it inside.

Step 5: Adjust the temperature to 175 °C to preheat for 5 minutes and press the "Start/Pause" button to start preheating.

Step 6: After preheating, place the chicken thighs into the preheated air fryer basket.

Step 7: Slide the basket inside and set the timer for 20 minutes.

Step 8: Press the "Start/Pause" button to start cooking.

Step 9: After 10 minutes of cooking, press the "Start/Pause" button to pause cooking and flip the chicken thighs.

Step 10: Again, press the "Start/Pause" button to resume cooking.

Step 11: After the cooking time has elapsed, remove the chicken thighs from the air fryer and serve hot alongside the lemon slices.

Serving Suggestion: Serve these chicken thighs with broccoli mash.

Crispy Chicken Thighs

Prep. Time
15 minutes

Cook. Time
20 minutes

Yield
3 Servings

A most amazing and satisfying chicken thighs recipe prepared in an air fryer! This air-fried recipe prepares chicken thighs with a crispy outside and an amazingly juicy inside. Crispy-skin chicken thighs are a perfect choice for a picnic or an impromptu event.

Energy value 241 Kcal | Protein 27.7g
Carbohydrates 20.6g | Fats 5g

Ingredients:

- 1 green onion, finely chopped
- 1 garlic clove, minced
- 10ml soy sauce
- 10ml rice vinegar
- 5g white sugar
- Salt and ground black pepper, as required
- 3x115g skinless, boneless chicken thighs
- 70g cornflour
- Non-stick cooking spray

Instructions:

Step 1: In a large bowl, mix together all the ingredients in a bowl except for the chicken thighs and cornflour.

Step 2: Add the chicken thighs and generously coat with the vinegar mixture.

Step 3: Add the cornflour in another bowl.

Step 4: Remove the chicken thighs from vinegar mixture and coat with cornflour.

Step 5: Grease the air fryer basket with cooking spray, then slide it inside.

Step 6: Adjust the temperature to 90 °C to preheat for 5 minutes and press the "Start/Pause" button to start preheating.

Step 7: After preheating, place the chicken thighs into the preheated air fryer basket, skin-side down.

Step 8: Slide the basket inside and set the timer for 10 minutes.

Step 9: Press the "Start/Pause" button to start cooking.

Step 10: After 10 minutes of cooking, immediately adjust the temperature to 180 °C for 10 minutes.

Step 11: After the cooking time has elapsed, remove the chicken thighs from the air fryer and serve hot.

Serving Suggestion: Enjoy these thighs with your favourite dipping sauce.

Oat-Crusted Chicken Breasts

Prep. Time
15 minutes

Cook. Time
12 minutes

Yield
2 Servings

One of the best chicken recipes for your dining table… This flavourful coating of oats, mustard powder, and fresh parsley makes chicken breasts deliciously crispy. These flavourful crispy chicken breasts are sure to be a hit with toddlers and adults alike.

Energy value 429 Kcal | Protein 45.1g
Carbohydrates 29.8g | Fats 13.8g

Ingredients:

• 2x150g chicken breasts
• Salt and ground black pepper, as required
• 75g oats
• 20–30g mustard powder
• 2g fresh parsley
• 2 medium eggs
• Non-stick cooking spray

Instructions:

Step 1: In a large bowl, mix together all the ingredients in a bowl except for the Step 1: Place the chicken breasts onto a chopping board, and with a meat mallet, flatten each into even thickness.Then cut each breast in half.

Step 2: Sprinkle the chicken pieces with salt and black pepper, then set aside.

Step 3: In a blender, add the oats, mustard powder, parsley, salt, and black pepper, and pulse until a coarse breadcrumb-like mixture is formed. Transfer the oat mixture into a shallow bowl.

Step 4: In another bowl, crack the eggs and beat well.

Step 5: Coat the chicken with the oats mixture, then dip into the beaten eggs. Coat again with the oats mixture.

Step 6: Grease the air fryer basket with cooking spray, then slide it inside. Adjust the temperature to 175 °C to preheat for 5 minutes and press the "Start/Pause" button to start preheating.

Step 7: After preheating, place the chicken breasts into the preheated air fryer basket in a single layer. Slide the basket inside and set the timer for 12 minutes. Press the "Start/Pause" button to start cooking.

Step 8: After 6 minutes of cooking, press the "Start/Pause" button to pause cooking. Flip the chicken breasts and press the "Start/Pause" button to resume cooking. After the cooking time has elapsed, remove the chicken breasts from the air fryer and serve hot.

Serving Suggestion: Serve these chicken breasts with a fresh green salad.

Parmesan Chicken Breast

Prep. Time
15 minutes

Cook. Time
20 minutes

Yield
3 Servings

Comfort food that is packed full of flavour… This is one of the best ways to prepare a dinner of tender and juicy chicken breast topped with gooey and crispy cheese. The combo of Parmesan cheese, pasta sauce, and basil intensify the flavour of chicken breast.

Energy value 593 Kcal | Protein 59.1g
Carbohydrates 28.2g | Fats 26.5g

Ingredients:

• 1 egg, beaten
• 30ml vegetable oil
• 115g breadcrumbs
• 5g fresh basil, chopped
• 3x170g chicken breasts
• Non-stick cooking spray
• 55g pasta sauce
• 30g Parmesan cheese, grated

Instructions:

Step 1: In a shallow bowl, beat the egg.

Step 2: In another bowl, add the oil, breadcrumbs, and basil, and mix until a crumbly mixture forms.

Step 3: Dip each chicken breast into the beaten egg, then coat with the breadcrumb mixture.

Step 4: Grease the air fryer basket with cooking spray, then slide it inside.

Step 5: Adjust the temperature to 175 °C to preheat for 5 minutes and press the "Start/Pause" button to start preheating.

Step 6: After preheating, place the chicken breasts into the preheated basket.

Step 7: Slide the basket into the air fryer, and set the timer for 20 minutes.

Step 8: After 15 minutes of cooking, press the "Start/Pause" button to pause cooking.

Step 9: Spoon the pasta sauce over the chicken breasts evenly and sprinkle with cheese.

Step 10: Again, press the "Start/Pause" button to resume cooking.

Step 11: After the cooking time has elapsed, remove the chicken breasts from the air fryer and serve hot.

Serving Suggestion: Enjoy these breasts with your favourite pasta.

Bacon-Wrapped Chicken Breasts

Prep. Time
15 minutes

Cook. Time
25 minutes

Yield
4 Servings

A recipe of extra juicy chicken breasts wrapped with delightfully smoky bacon... These bacon-wrapped chicken breasts are seasoned with a combo of basil, palm sugar, and fish sauce, and then cooked in the air fryer until caramelised. You'll be sure to receive huge appreciation from your family and friends.

Energy value 365 Kcal | Protein 30.2g
Carbohydrates 2.7g | Fats 24.9g

Ingredients:

- 10g palm sugar
- 6–7 fresh basil leaves
- 30ml fish sauce
- 30ml water
- 2x226g chicken breasts, cut each breast in half horizontally
- Salt and ground black pepper, as required
- 12 bacon strips
- 10g honey
- Non-stick cooking spray

Instructions:

Step 1: In a small heavy-bottomed pan, add palm sugar over medium-low heat and cook for about 2–3 minutes or until caramelised, stirring continuously. Add the basil, fish sauce, and water, then stir to combine.

Step 2: Remove from the heat and transfer the sugar mixture into a large bowl. Sprinkle each chicken breast with salt and black pepper. Add the chicken pieces into the bowl of sugar mixture and coat well.

Step 3: Refrigerate to marinate for about 4–6 hours.

Step 4: Wrap each chicken piece with 3 bacon strips. Slightly coat each piece with honey.

Step 5: Grease the air fryer basket with cooking spray, then slide it inside. Adjust the temperature to 185 °C to preheat for 5 minutes and press the "Start/Pause" button to start preheating.

Step 6: After preheating, place the chicken pieces into the preheated air fryer basket. Slide the basket inside and set the timer for 20 minutes. Press the "Start/Pause" button to start cooking.

Step 7: After 10 minutes of cooking, press the "Start/Pause" button to pause cooking. Flip the chicken pieces and press the "Start/Pause" button to resume cooking.

Step 8: After the cooking time has elapsed, remove the chicken pieces from the air fryer and serve hot.

Serving Suggestion: Enjoy this bacon-wrapped chicken breast with a side of lemon rice.

Spinach-Stuffed Chicken Breasts

Prep. Time
15 minutes

Cook. Time
30 minutes

Yield
2 Servings

A winner and elegant recipe of chicken breasts that will instantly upgrade your dinner menu... These tender and juicy chicken breasts are stuffed with a cheesy spinach filling and topped with cheddar cheese. This flavourful meal will be great for gatherings of family and friends.

Energy value 281 Kcal | Protein 31.6g
Carbohydrates 2.9g | Fats 16.1g

Ingredients:

- 15ml olive oil
- 55g fresh spinach
- 55g ricotta cheese, grated
- 2x115g skinless, boneless chicken breasts
- Salt and ground black pepper, as required
- 20g cheddar cheese, grated
- 1.25g paprika
- Non-stick cooking spray

Instructions:

Step 1: In a medium skillet, add the oil over medium heat and cook until heated.

Step 2: Add the spinach and cook for about 3–4 minutes.

Step 3: Stir in the ricotta and cook for about 40–60 seconds.

Step 4: Remove the skillet from the heat and set aside to cool.

Step 5: Cut slits into the chicken breasts about ¼-inch apart but not all the way through.

Step 6: Stuff each chicken breast with the spinach mixture.

Step 7: Sprinkle each chicken breast with salt and black pepper.

Step 8: Then sprinkle with cheddar cheese and paprika.

Step 9: Grease the air fryer basket with cooking spray, then slide it inside.

Step 10: Adjust the temperature to 190 °C to preheat for 5 minutes and press the "Start/Pause" button to start preheating.

Step 11: After preheating, place chicken breasts into the preheated basket. Slide the basket inside and set the timer for 20–25 minutes. Press the "Start/Pause" button to start cooking.

Step 12: After the cooking time has elapsed, remove the chicken breasts from the air fryer and serve hot.

Serving Suggestion: Seve alongside creamy potato salad.

Chicken Kebabs

Prep. Time
15 minutes

Cook. Time
15 minutes

Yield
4 Servings

Fun-to-eat chicken kebabs for the whole family… Use one of the unique ways to prepare chicken kebabs without the use of a smoky outdoor grill… You can easily prepare delicious chicken kebabs in an air fryer with ease. These chicken kebabs are packed with the deliciousness of spices and yoghurt.

Energy value 201 Kcal | Protein 29.1g
Carbohydrates 2.9g | Fats 8.1g

Ingredients:

- 455g skinless, boneless chicken thighs, cut into cubes
- 125g plain Greek yoghurt
- 15ml olive oil
- 10g curry powder
- 2.5g smoked paprika
- 1.25g cayenne powder
- Salt, as required
- Non-stick cooking spray

Instructions:

Step 1: In a bowl, add the chicken, oil, yoghurt, and spices, and mix until well combined.

Step 2: Refrigerate to marinate for about 2 hours.

Step 3: Thread the chicken cubes onto pre-soaked wooden skewers.

Step 4: Grease the air fryer basket with cooking spray, then slide it inside.

Step 5: Adjust the temperature to 185 °C to preheat for 5 minutes and press the "Start/Pause" button to start preheating.

Step 6: After preheating, place the chicken skewers into the preheated air fryer basket.

Step 7: Slide the basket inside and set the timer for 15 minutes.

Step 8: Press the "Start/Pause" button to start cooking.

Step 9: After the cooking time has elapsed, remove the chicken skewers from the air fryer and serve hot.

Serving Suggestion: Serve these kebabs with fresh greens.

Crispy Chicken Burgers

Prep. Time
20 minutes

Cook. Time
10 minutes

Yield
4 Servings

One of the best recipes to prepare restaurant-style crispy chicken burgers at home… These ultra-crispy chicken burgers are bursting with delicious flavours. The ground chicken is seasoned with mustard, paprika, and Worcestershire sauce, then coated with a crispy topping of flour and flavourful breadcrumbs.

Energy value 445 Kcal | Protein 46.9g
Carbohydrates 41.8g | Fats 9.7g

Ingredients:

- 4x140g boneless, skinless chicken breasts
- 5g mustard powder
- 2.5g paprika
- 5ml Worcestershire sauce
- 35g plain flour
- 1 small egg
- 60g breadcrumbs
- 1.25g dried parsley
- 1.25g dried tarragon
- 1.25g dried oregano
- 5g dried garlic
- 5g chicken seasoning
- 2.5g cayenne powder
- Salt and ground black pepper, as required
- 4 hamburger buns, split and toasted
- 4 lettuce leaves
- 4 mozzarella cheese slices

Instructions:

Step 1: In a food processor, add the chicken breasts and pulse until minced. Add the mustard, paprika, Worcestershire sauce, salt, and black pepper, and pulse until well combined. Make 4 equal-sized patties from the mixture.

Step 2: In a shallow bowl, place the flour. In a second bowl, crack the egg and beat well. In a third bowl, mix the breadcrumbs, dried herbs, and spices. Coat each chicken patty with flour and dip into the egg. Then coat with the breadcrumb mixture.

Step 3: Grease the air fryer basket with cooking spray, then slide it inside. Adjust the temperature to 185 °C to preheat for 5 minutes and press the "Start/Pause" button to start preheating.

Step 4: After preheating, place the patties into the preheated air fryer basket. Slide the basket inside and set the timer for 10 minutes. Press the "Start/Pause" button to start cooking.

Step 5: After 5 minutes of cooking, press the "Start/Pause" button to pause cooking. Flip the patties and press the "Start/Pause" button to resume cooking. After the cooking time has elapsed, remove the patties from the air fryer and place onto a plate.

Step 6: Place one lettuce leaf over the bottom half of each bun, followed by one patty and cheese slice. Cover with the bun top and serve.

Serving Suggestion: Serve these burgers with honey mustard coleslaw.

Simple Turkey Breast

Prep. Time
10 minutes

Cook. Time
45 minutes

Yield
10 Servings

A gourmet and awesome treat for Sunday dinners… You can prepare this turkey breast in an air fryer without any fuss. This simple and easy air fryer recipe prepares roasted turkey breast with crispy skin and tender, juicy meat. Your whole family is going to love this turkey breast.

Energy value 720 Kcal | Protein 97.2g
Carbohydrates 0g | Fats 9g

Ingredients:

- Non-stick cooking spray
- 1 bone-in turkey breast (640g)
- Salt and ground black pepper, as required
- 30ml olive oil

Instructions:

Step 1: Grease the air fryer basket with cooking spray, then slide it inside.

Step 2: Adjust the temperature to 180 °C to preheat for 5 minutes and press the "Start/Pause" button to start preheating.

Step 3: Sprinkle the turkey breast with salt and black pepper, then drizzle with oil.

Step 4: After preheating, place the turkey breast into the preheated air fryer basket, skin-side down.

Step 5: Slide the basket inside and set the timer for 45 minutes.

Step 6: Press the "Start/Pause" button to start cooking.

Step 7: After 20 minutes of cooking, press the "Start/Pause" button to pause cooking, flip the turkey breast.

Step 8: Again, press the "Start/Pause" button to resume cooking.

Step 9: After the cooking time has elapsed, remove the turkey breast from the air fryer and place onto a chopping board for about 10 minutes before slicing.

Step 10: Cut the turkey breast into slices of the desired size and serve.

Serving Suggestion: Serve with cranberry sauce and creamed corn.

.

Herbed Turkey Breast

Prep. Time
10 minutes

Cook. Time
35 minutes

Yield
6 Servings

A lavish and full-of-flavour dinner recipe of turkey breast for special occasions… Surely this turkey breast will fill your home with a delicious herby aroma. The dried herbs, brown sugar, and spices are the key ingredients of flavouring the turkey breast.

Energy value 349 Kcal | Protein 40.7g
Carbohydrates 1.8 | Fats 16g

Ingredients:

- 1.5g dried rosemary, crushed
- 1.5g dried thyme, crushed
- 1.5g dried sage, crushed
- 5g dark brown sugar
- 2.5g paprika
- 2.5g garlic powder
- Salt and ground black pepper, as required
- 1 bone-in, skin-on turkey breast (1.13kg)
- 15ml olive oil
- Non-stick cooking spray

Instructions:

Step 1: In a bowl, mix together the herbs, brown sugar, and spices.

Step 2: Coat the turkey breast evenly with oil and generously rub with the herb mixture.

Step 3: Grease the air fryer basket with cooking spray, then slide it inside.

Step 4: Adjust the temperature to 185 °C to preheat for 5 minutes and press the "Start/Pause" button to start preheating.

Step 5: After preheating, place the turkey breast into the preheated air fryer basket, skin-side down.

Step 6: Slide the basket inside and set the timer for 35 minutes. Press the "Start/Pause" button to start cooking.

Step 7: After 18 minutes of cooking, press the "Start/Pause" button to pause cooking.

Step 8: Flip the turkey breast and press the "Start/Pause" button to resume cooking.

Step 9: After the cooking time has elapsed, remove the turkey breast from the air fryer and place onto a chopping board for about 10 minutes before slicing.

Step 10: Cut the turkey breast into slices of the desired size and serve.

Serving Suggestion: Serve with cranberry sauce and creamed corn.

Zesty Turkey Legs

Prep. Time
10 minutes

Cook. Time
30 minutes

Yield
2 Servings

Feeling the pressure to roast turkey legs for your dinner? Here is an air fryer recipe of moist and flavourful turkey legs with a hint of zesty lime… These air-fried turkey legs will be a great addition to your menu to celebrate special occasions.

Energy value 458 Kcal | Protein 44.6g
Carbohydrates 2.3g | Fats 29.5g

Ingredients:

- 2 garlic cloves, minced
- 2g fresh rosemary, minced
- 3g fresh lime zest, finely grated
- 30ml olive oil
- 15ml fresh lime juice
- Salt and ground black pepper, as required
- 2 turkey legs
- Non-stick cooking spray

Instructions:

Step 1: In a large bowl, mix together the garlic, rosemary, lime zest, oil, lime juice, salt, and black pepper.

Step 2: Add the turkey legs and generously coat with the marinade.

Step 3: Refrigerate to marinate for about 6–8 hours.

Step 4: Grease the air fryer basket with cooking spray, then slide it inside.

Step 5: Adjust the temperature to 175 °C to preheat for 5 minutes and press the "Start/Pause" button to start preheating.

Step 6: After preheating, place the turkey legs into the preheated air fryer basket.

Step 7: Slide the basket inside and set the timer for 30 minutes.

Step 8: Press the "Start/Pause" button to start cooking.

Step 9: After 15 minutes of cooking, press the "Start/Pause" button to pause cooking.

Step 10: Flip the turkey legs and press the "Start/Pause" button to resume cooking.

Step 11: After the cooking time has elapsed, remove the turkey legs from the air fryer and serve hot.

Serving Suggestion: Serve alongside steamed green beans.

Turkey Meatloaf

Prep. Time
15 minutes

Cook. Time
20 minutes

Yield
4 Servings

Are you set ready to create one of the best turkey meatloaves? Here is an air fryer recipe! This Mexican-inspired meatloaf recipe comprises great texture and taste… The combo of cheese, salsa verde, green chillies, kale, breadcrumbs, and spices enhances the flavour of the meatloaf.

Energy value 429 Kcal | Protein 36.9g
Carbohydrates 33.5g | Fats 18g

Ingredients:

- 455g ground turkey
- 55g fresh kale, trimmed and finely chopped
- 50g onion, chopped
- 1 can chopped green chillies (115g)
- 5g fresh coriander, chopped
- 2 garlic cloves, minced
- 1 egg, beaten
- 115g cheddar cheese, grated
- 65g salsa verde
- 50g fresh breadcrumbs
- 2.5g dried oregano, crushed
- 5g red chilli powder
- 2.5g ground cumin
- Salt and ground black pepper, as required

Instructions:

Step 1: In a deep bowl, place all the ingredients, and with your hands, mix until well combined.

Step 2: Divide the turkey mixture into 4 equal-sized portions and shape each into a mini loaf.

Step 3: Grease the air fryer basket with cooking spray, then slide it inside.

Step 4: Adjust the temperature to 205 °C to preheat for 5 minutes and press the "Start/Pause" button to start preheating.

Step 5: After preheating, place the loaves into the preheated air fryer basket.

Step 6: Slide the basket inside and set the timer for 20 minutes.

Step 7: Press the "Start/Pause" button to start cooking.

Step 8: After the cooking time has elapsed, remove the loaves from the air fryer and place onto plates for about 5 minutes before serving.

Step 9: Serve warm.

Serving Suggestion: Serve with fresh veggie salad.

Glazed Duck Breast

Prep. Time
15 minutes

Cook. Time
44 minutes

Yield
3 Servings

A recipe of aromatic and deliciously glazed duck breast with a light, crispy, tender, and juicy texture... The flavour-packed glaze of pomegranate juice, lemon juice, and brown sugar is the base of deliciousness in this duck breast dish. This is a great choice for weeknight dinners.

Energy value 315 Kcal | Protein 33.5g
Carbohydrates 29.3g | Fats 6.2g

Ingredients:

- 480ml fresh pomegranate juice
- 30ml lemon juice
- 40g brown sugar
- 455g boneless duck breast
- Salt and ground black pepper, as required
- Non-stick cooking spray

Instructions:

Step 1: In a medium saucepan, add the pomegranate juice, lemon juice, and brown sugar over medium heat, and bring to a boil.

Step 2: Now adjust the heat to low and cook for about 25 minutes or until the mixture becomes thick.

Step 3: Remove the pan from the heat and let it cool slightly.

Step 4: Score the fat of the duck breast several times using a sharp knife.

Step 5: Sprinkle the duck breast with salt and black pepper.

Step 6: Grease the air fryer basket with cooking spray, then slide it inside.

Step 7: Adjust the temperature to 205 °C to preheat for 5 minutes and press the "Start/Pause" button to start preheating.

Step 8: After preheating, place the duck breast into the preheated air fryer basket, skin-side up.

Step 9: Slide the basket inside and set the timer for 14 minutes. Press the "Start/Pause" button to start cooking.

Step 10: After 7 minutes of cooking, press the "Start/Pause" button to pause cooking.

Step 11: Flip the duck breast and press the "Start/Pause" button to resume cooking.

Step 12: After the cooking time has elapsed, remove the duck breast from the air fryer and place onto a chopping board for about 5–10 minutes.

Step 13: Cut the duck breast into slices of the desired size and transfer onto serving plates. Drizzle with warm pomegranate juice mixture and serve.

Serving Suggestion: Serve alongside sautéed bok choy.

Herbed Duck Legs

Prep. Time
10 minutes

Cook. Time
30 minutes

Yield
2 Servings

One of the greatest ways to prepare duck legs with flavour... This air fryer recipe prepares a dinner of perfectly cooked duck legs, with crispy skin and succulent meat. These Chinese-style duck legs are infused with the flavourful combo of garlic, fresh herbs, and five-spice powder.

Energy value 140 Kcal | Protein 25g
Carbohydrates 1g | Fats 4.5g

Ingredients:

- 1 garlic clove, minced
- 2g fresh thyme, chopped
- 2g fresh oregano, chopped
- 2g fresh parsley, chopped
- 5g five-spice powder
- Salt and ground black pepper, as required
- 2 duck legs
- Non-stick cooking spray

Instructions:

Step 1: In a bowl, add the garlic, herbs, five-spice powder, salt, and black pepper, and mix until well combined.

Step 2: Rub the duck legs with the garlic mixture generously.

Step 3: Set aside for about 10–15 minutes.

Step 4: Grease the air fryer basket with cooking spray, then slide it inside.

Step 5: Adjust the temperature to 165 °C to preheat for 5 minutes and press the "Start/Pause" button to start preheating.

Step 6: After preheating, place the duck legs into the preheated air fryer basket.

Step 7: Slide the basket inside and set the timer for 30 minutes.

Step 8: Press the "Start/Pause" button to start cooking.

Step 9: After 15 minutes of cooking, press the "Start/Pause" button to pause cooking.

Step 10: Flip the duck legs and press the "Start/Pause" button to resume cooking.

Step 11: After the cooking time has elapsed, remove the duck legs from the air fryer and serve hot.

Serving Suggestion: Serve alongside sautéed mushrooms.

Beef Recipes

Hello! Please scan the QR code below to access your promised bonus of all our recipes with full colored photos & beautiful designs! It is the best we could do to keep the book as cheap as possible while providing the best value!

Also, once downloaded you can take the PDF with you digitally wherever you go- meaning you can cook these recipes wherever an Air Fryer is present!

STEP BY STEP Guide To Access-

1) Open Your Phones (Or Any Device You Want The Book On) Back Camera. The Back Camera Is The One You use as if you are taking a picture of someone.

2) Simply point your Camera at the QR code and 'tap' the QR code with your finger to focus the camera.

3) A link / pop up will appear. Simply tap that (and make sure you have internet connection) and the FREE PDF containing all of the colored images should appear.

4) If You Click On The File And It Says 'The File Is Too Big To Preview' Simply click 'Download' and it will download the full book onto your phone!

5) Now you have access to these FOREVER. Simply 'Bookmark' The tab it opened on, or download the document and take wherever you want.

6) Repeat this on any device you want it on!

Any Issues / Feedback / Troubleshooting please email: anthonypublishing123@gmail.com and our customer service team will help you! We want to make sure you have the BEST experience with our books!

Buttered Filet Mignon

Prep. Time
10 minutes

Cook. Time
14 minutes

Yield
2 Servings

A super-quick and easy dish for an elegant dinner… This easy-to-prepare and simple filet mignon with butter tastes phenomenal! A coating of butter, salt, and black pepper gives a deliciously tender and juicy profile to the filet mignon.

Energy value 355 Kcal I Protein 47.8g
Carbohydrates 0g I Fats 17g

Ingredients:

- Non-stick cooking spray
- 2x170g filet mignon
- Salt and ground black pepper, as required
- 20g butter, softened

Instructions:

Step 1: Grease the air fryer basket with cooking spray, then slide it inside.

Step 2: Adjust the temperature to 200 °C to preheat for 5 minutes and press the "Start/Pause" button to start preheating.

Step 3: Press the "Start/Pause" button to start preheating.

Step 4: Coat both sides of the fillet with butter, then season with salt and black pepper.

Step 5: After preheating, place the fillet into the preheated air fryer basket.

Step 6: Slide the basket inside and set the timer for 14 minutes.

Step 7: Press the "Start/Pause" button to start cooking.

Step 8: After 7 minutes of cooking, press the "Start/Pause" button to pause cooking.

Step 9: Flip the fillet and press the "Start/Pause" button to resume cooking.

Step 10: After the cooking time has elapsed, remove the fillet from the air fryer and serve hot.

Serving Suggestion: Serve with steamed veggies.

Bacon-Wrapped Filet Mignon

Prep. Time
10 minutes

Cook. Time
15 minutes

Yield
2 Servings

An elegant and surprisingly delicious filet mignon wrapped in bacon and cooked to perfection in an air fryer! This recipe is a perfect choice for Valentine's Day dinners. This impressive and delicious restaurant-style filet mignon is easy to make at home!

Energy value 428 Kcal I Protein 52.9g
Carbohydrates 0.5g I Fats 22.3g

Ingredients:

- 2 bacon slices
- 2x150g filet mignon
- Salt and ground black pepper, as required
- 5ml avocado oil
- Non-stick cooking spray

Instructions:

Step 1: Wrap 1 bacon slice around each fillet and secure with a cocktail stick.

Step 2: Season the steak evenly with salt and black pepper.

Step 3: Coat each steak with avocado oil.

Step 4: Grease the air fryer basket with cooking spray, then slide it inside.

Step 5: Adjust the temperature of the air fryer to 190 °C to preheat for 5 minutes and press the "Start/Pause" button to start preheating.

Step 6: After preheating, place the fillets into the preheated air fryer basket.

Step 7: Slide the basket inside and set the timer for 15 minutes.

Step 8: Press the "Start/Pause" button to start cooking.

Step 9: After 8 minutes of cooking, press the "Start/Pause" button to pause cooking.

Step 10: Flip the fillets and press the "Start/Pause" button to resume cooking.

Step 11: After the cooking time has elapsed, remove the fillets from the air fryer and serve hot.

Serving Suggestion: Serve alongside loaded baked potatoes.

Glazed Beef Short Ribs

Prep. Time
10 minutes

Cook. Time
16 minutes

Yield
4 Servings

A pretty much foolproof dinner dish of Asian-inspired beef short ribs for gatherings and parties… This sweet and zesty glaze transforms the short ribs and gives them a rich, irresistible taste. This air fryer recipe prepares beef short ribs in less time when compared to an oven.

Energy value 496 Kcal I Protein 67.7g
Carbohydrates 6.5g I Fats 20.5g

Ingredients:

- 1kg bone-in beef short ribs
- 5g fresh ginger, finely grated
- 60ml balsamic vinegar
- 15g sugar
- 1 green onion, chopped
- 120ml light soy sauce
- 10ml sriracha
- 2.5g ground black pepper
- Non-stick cooking spray

Instructions:

Step 1: Grease the air fryer basket with cooking spray, then slide it inside.

Step 2: Adjust the temperature of the air fryer to 195 °C to preheat for 5 minutes and press the "Start/Pause" button to start preheating.

Step 3: After preheating, place the ribs into the preheated air fryer basket.

Step 4: Slide the basket inside and set the timer for 16 minutes.

Step 5: Press the "Start/Pause" button to start cooking.

Step 6: After 8 minutes of cooking, press the "Start/Pause" button to pause cooking.

Step 7: Flip the ribs and press the "Start/Pause" button to resume cooking.

Step 8: After the cooking time has elapsed, remove the ribs from the air fryer and serve hot.

Serving Suggestion: Serve with macaroni salad.

Spicy Round Roast

Prep. Time
10 minutes

Cook. Time
50 minutes

Yield
8 Servings

An incredibly tender and flavourful round roast… Prepare this delicious and tender cut of beef round roast with little effort and care in your air fryer. A simple spice blend and oil are the main agents which add to the deliciousness of this round roast.

Energy value 264 Kcal I Protein 41.8g
Carbohydrates 0.9g I Fats 9.4g

Ingredients:

- Non-stick cooking spray
- 30ml olive oil
- 2.5g garlic powder
- 2.5g onion powder
- 2.5g cayenne powder
- 2.5g ground black pepper
- Salt, as required
- 1.13kg beef round roast, trimmed

Instructions:

Step 1: Grease the air fryer basket with cooking spray, then slide it inside.

Step 2: Adjust the temperature of the air fryer to 185 °C to preheat for 5 minutes and press the "Start/Pause" button to start preheating.

Step 3: In a bowl, mix together the oil and spices.

Step 4: Coat the roast with spice mixture evenly.

Step 5: After preheating, place the roast into the preheated air fryer basket.

Step 6: Slide the basket inside and set the timer for 50 minutes.

Step 7: Press the "Start/Pause" button to start cooking.

Step 8: After the cooking time has elapsed, remove the roast from the air fryer and place onto a platter.

Step 9: With a piece of foil, cover the roast for about 10 minutes before slicing.

Step 10: Cut the roast into slices of the desired size and serve.

Serving Suggestion: Serve alongside corn salad. .

Herbed Beef Chuck Roast

Prep. Time
10 minutes

Cook. Time
50 minutes

Yield
6 Servings

One of the best ways to prepare chuck roast in a simple but delicious way… You will definitely love making this recipe again and again. This succulent and mouthwatering chuck roast will thrill your family and guests alike at a dinner party.

Energy value 406 Kcal | Protein 47.2g
Carbohydrates 1.1g | Fats 22.4g

Ingredients:

- Non-stick cooking spray
- 910g beef chuck roast
- 15ml olive oil
- 5g dried rosemary, crushed
- 5g dried thyme, crushed
- 5g dried parsley, crushed
- Salt, as required

Instructions:

Step 1: Grease the air fryer basket with cooking spray, then slide it inside.

Step 2: Adjust the temperature of the air fryer to 185 °C to preheat for 5 minutes and press the "Start/Pause" button to start preheating.

Step 3: In a bowl, mix together the oil, herbs, and salt.

Step 4: Generously coat the roast with the herb mixture.

Step 5: After preheating, place the roast into the preheated air fryer basket.

Step 6: Slide the basket inside and set the timer for 45 minutes.

Step 7: Press the "Start/Pause" button to start cooking.

Step 8: After the cooking time has elapsed, remove the roast from the air fryer and place onto a platter.

Step 9: With a piece of foil, cover the roast for about 10 minutes before slicing.

Step 10: Cut the roast into slices of the desired size and serve.

Serving Suggestion: Serve alongside baked beans.

Simple Rib-Eye Steak

Prep. Time
10 minutes

Cook. Time
14 minutes

Yield
4 Servings

An air fryer recipe of rib-eye steak that tastes divine… This dish doesn't require a lot of time and ingredients for cooking. Cooking in an air fryer achieves the perfect taste and texture of rib-eye steak at the best temperature. This recipe will suit those who follow a healthy lifestyle!

Energy value 340 Kcal | Protein 20g
Carbohydrates 0g | Fats 28.6g

Ingredients:

- Non-stick cooking spray
- 2x226g rib-eye steaks
- Salt and ground black pepper, as required
- 15ml olive oil

Instructions:

Step 1: Grease the air fryer basket with cooking spray, then slide it inside.

Step 2: Adjust the temperature of the air fryer to 205 °C to preheat for 5 minutes and press the "Start/Pause" button to start preheating.

Step 3: Coat the steak evenly with oil, then sprinkle with salt and black pepper.

Step 4: After preheating, place the steaks into the preheated air fryer basket.

Step 5: Slide the basket inside and set the timer for 14 minutes.

Step 6: Press the "Start/Pause" button to start cooking.

Step 7: After 15 minutes of cooking, press the "Start/Pause" button to pause cooking.

Step 8: Flip the steaks and press the "Start/Pause" button to resume cooking.

Step 9: After the cooking time has elapsed, remove the steaks from the air fryer and place onto a platter for about 5 minutes.

Step 10: Cut each steak into slices of the desired size and serve.

Serving Suggestion: Serve with sweet potato mash.

Buttered Striploin Steak

Prep. Time
10 minutes

Cook. Time
12 minutes

Yield
2 Servings

A perfectly done plate of juicy, tender, and delicious steak for the dinner table… This striploin steak recipe requires only a few ingredients which can be added in any amount without any fuss. The coating of butter, salt, and black pepper add a perfect deliciousness to this steak.

Energy value 598 Kcal I Protein 57.4g
Carbohydrates 0g I Fats 39.4g

Ingredients:

- Non-stick cooking spray
- 2x200g striploin steak
- 30g butter, softened
- Salt and ground black pepper, as required

Instructions:

Step 1: Grease the air fryer basket with cooking spray, then slide it inside.

Step 2: Adjust the temperature to 200 °C to preheat for 5 minutes and press the "Start/Pause" button to start preheating.

Step 3: Coat each steak evenly with butter, then season with salt and black pepper.

Step 4: After preheating, place the steaks into the preheated air fryer basket.

Step 5: Slide the basket inside and set the timer for 8–12 minutes.

Step 6: Press the "Start/Pause" button to start cooking.

Step 7: After the cooking time has elapsed, remove the steaks from the air fryer and serve hot.

Serving Suggestion: Serve alongside chickpea salad.

Spiced and Herbed Skirt Steak

Prep. Time
15 minutes

Cook. Time
10 minutes

Yield
4 Servings

A loveable and simply delicious recipe of skirt steak for dinner… This divine marinade of fresh herbs and spices gives juicy skirt steaks an amazingly delicious flavour. This wonderful air fryer recipe of steak is perfect for special family meals.

Energy value 312 Kcal I Protein 30.9g
Carbohydrates 3.5g I Fats 19.2g

Ingredients:

- 2 garlic cloves, minced
- 5g fresh parsley leaves, finely chopped
- 5g fresh oregano, finely chopped
- 5g fresh mint leaves, finely chopped
- 5g ground cumin
- 5g smoked paprika
- 5g cayenne powder
- 5g red pepper flakes, crushed
- Salt and ground black pepper, as required
- 30ml olive oil
- 30ml red wine vinegar
- 2x225g skirt steaks
- Non-stick cooking spray

Instructions:

Step 1: In a bowl, mix together the garlic, herbs, spices, oil, and vinegar.

Step 2: In a resealable bag, place ¼ of the herb mixture and steaks. Seal the bag and shake to coat well.

Step 3: Refrigerate for about 24 hours.

Step 4: Remove the steaks from the refrigerator and leave at room temperature for about 30 minutes.

Step 5: Grease the air fryer basket with cooking spray, then slide it inside. Adjust the temperature to 200 °C to preheat for 5 minutes and press the "Start/Pause" button to start preheating.

Step 6: Coat each steak evenly with butter, then season with salt and black pepper.

Step 7: After preheating, place the steaks into the preheated air fryer basket. Place the steaks into the preheated air fryer basket. Slide the basket inside and set the timer for 8–10 minutes. Press the "Start/Pause" button to start cooking.

Step 8: After the cooking time has elapsed, remove the steaks from the air fryer and place onto a chopping board for about 10 minutes before slicing.

Step 9: Cut each steak into slices of the desired size & serve.

Serving Suggestion: Serve with garlicky green beans.

Seasoned New York Strip Steak

Prep. Time
10 minutes

Cook. Time
8 minutes

Yield
2 Servings

An elegant and classic recipe of New York strip steak… You can prepare this cut of steak without many ingredients. This perfect and fantastic mix of steak seasoning, salt, and black pepper adds a deliciously spicy flavouring to this steak.

Energy value 279 Kcal | Protein 37.6g
Carbohydrates 0g | Fats 13.1g

Ingredients:

- Non-stick cooking spray
- 1 New York strip steak (270g)
- 15g steak seasoning
- Salt and ground black pepper, as required
- 10g butter, melted

Instructions:

Step 1: Grease the air fryer basket with cooking spray, then slide it inside.

Step 2: Adjust the temperature to 205 °C to preheat for 5 minutes and press the "Start/Pause" button to start preheating.

Step 3: Coat the steak with oil, then generously season with salt and black pepper.

Step 4: After preheating, place the steak into the preheated air fryer basket.

Step 5: Slide the basket inside and set the timer for 8 minutes.

Step 6: Press the "Start/Pause" button to start cooking.

Step 7: After the cooking time has elapsed, remove the steak from the air fryer and place onto a chopping board for about 10 minutes before slicing.

Step 8: Cut the steak into slices of the desired size and transfer onto serving plates.

Serving Suggestion: Serve with coleslaw.

Crumbed Sirloin Steak

Prep. Time
15 minutes

Cook. Time
10 minutes

Yield
4 Servings

One of the best recipes for dinner… This recipe comprises a deliciously crispy steak with juicy and tender meat. Sirloin steak gets the royal treatment, first coated with flour, then dipped in eggs, and finally garnished with seasoned panko breadcrumbs.

Energy value 454 Kcal | Protein 37.2g
Carbohydrates 31.8g | Fats 10.6g

Ingredients:

- 130g white flour
- 2 eggs
- 120g panko breadcrumbs
- 5g onion powder
- 5g garlic powder
- 2.5g paprika
- Salt and ground black pepper, as required
- 4x170g sirloin steaks, pounded slightly
- Non-stick cooking spray

Instructions:

Step 1: In a shallow bowl, place the flour.

Step 2: Crack the eggs in a second bowl and beat well.

Step 3: In a third bowl, mix together the panko and spices.

Step 4: Coat each steak with the flour and dip into the beaten eggs. Then coat with the panko mixture.

Step 5: Grease the air fryer basket with cooking spray, then slide it inside.

Step 6: Adjust the temperature to 185 °C to preheat for 5 minutes and press the "Start/Pause" button to start preheating.

Step 7: After preheating, place the steaks into the preheated air fryer basket.

Step 8: Slide the basket inside and set the timer for 10 minutes.

Step 9: Press the "Start/Pause" button to start cooking.

Step 10: After the cooking time has elapsed, remove the steaks from the air fryer and serve immediately.

Serving Suggestion: Serve with creamed spinach.

Steak with Bell Peppers

Prep. Time
15 minutes

Cook. Time
11 minutes

Yield
4 Servings

Are you ready to sizzle? Then dress up your plate with a colourful and beautiful presentation on your dining table. Strips of flank steak, colourful bell peppers, onion, and seasoning make a tasty dish that the whole family will enjoy. This colourful meal of steak and bell peppers is super-delicious and hearty.

Energy value 233 Kcal | Protein 31.8g
Carbohydrates 9.8g | Fats 7.2g

Ingredients:

- 5g dried oregano, crushed
- 2.5g onion powder
- 2.5g garlic powder
- 2.5g red chilli powder
- 2.5g paprika
- Salt, to taste
- 400g beef flank steak, cut into thin strips
- 1 large green bell pepper, seeded and sliced
- 1 large red bell pepper, seeded and sliced
- 1 red onion, sliced
- 30ml olive oil
- Non-stick cooking spray

Instructions:

Step 1: In a large bowl, mix together the oregano and spices.

Step 2: Add the beef strips, bell peppers, onion, and oil, and mix until well combined.

Step 3: Grease the air fryer basket with cooking spray, then slide it inside.

Step 4: Adjust the temperature to 200 ºC to preheat for 5 minutes and press the "Start/Pause" button to start preheating.

Step 5: After preheating, place the steak mixture into the preheated air fryer basket.

Step 6: Slide the basket inside and set the timer for 11 minutes.

Step 7: Press the "Start/Pause" button to start cooking.

Step 8: After the cooking time has elapsed, remove the steak mixture from the air fryer and serve immediately.

Steak with Mushrooms

Prep. Time
15 minutes

Cook. Time
10 minutes

Yield
4 Servings

A simple meal of steak and mushrooms with a deliciously tasty twist of soy sauce and honey… Cooking in an air fryer will help you to prepare this hearty meal without any hassle. This dish is great for feeding your family and friends too.

Energy value 381 Kcal | Protein 30.9g
Carbohydrates 11.1g | Fats 24.6g

Ingredients:

- 60ml olive oil, divided
- 30ml soy sauce
- 30g honey
- 1 skirt steak, cut into thin strips (400g)
- 455g fresh mushrooms, quartered
- 2 green onions, sliced
- Salt and ground black pepper, as required

Instructions:

Step 1: In a bowl, mix together 30ml of oil, soy sauce, and honey.

Step 2: Add the steak strips and generously coat with the oil mixture.

Step 3: In another bowl, add the mushrooms, green onions, remaining oil, salt, and black pepper, and toss to coat well.

Step 4: Grease the air fryer basket with cooking spray, then slide it inside.

Step 5: Adjust the temperature to 200 ºC to preheat for 5 minutes and press the "Start/Pause" button to start preheating.

Step 6: After preheating, place the steak strips and mushroom mixture into the preheated air fryer basket.

Step 7: Slide the basket inside and set the timer for 10 minutes.

Step 8: Press the "Start/Pause" button to start cooking.

Step 9: After the cooking time has elapsed, remove the steak strips and mushroom mixture from the air fryer and serve hot.

Beef Cheeseburgers

Prep. Time
15 minutes

Cook. Time
12 minutes

Yield
2 Servings

The best and most delicious recipe of cheesy beef burgers for family feasts… These cheesy burgers are outrageously delicious and hearty. You can easily prepare a platter of scrumptious cheeseburgers in an air fryer for your family.

Energy value 497 Kcal I Protein 39.3g
Carbohydrates 19.1g I Fats 29.4g

Ingredients:

- 225g ground beef
- 1 garlic clove, minced
- 2g fresh coriander, minced
- Salt and ground black pepper, as required
- Non-stick cooking spray
- 2 cheddar cheese slices
- 2 burger buns, cut in half
- 2 lettuce leaves

Instructions:

Step 1: In a bowl, mix together the beef, garlic, coriander, salt, and black pepper.

Step 2: Make 2x4-inch patties from the mixture.

Step 3: Grease the air fryer pan with cooking spray, then slide it inside.

Step 4: Adjust the temperature to 200 °C to preheat for 5 minutes and press the "Start/Pause" button to start preheating.

Step 5: After preheating, place the patties into the preheated air fryer pan in a single layer.

Step 6: Slide the basket inside and set the timer for 12 minutes.

Step 7: Press the "Start/Pause" button to start cooking.

Step 8: After 11 minutes of cooking, press the "Start/Pause" button to pause cooking.

Step 9: Place 1 cheese slice over each patty and press the "Start/Pause" button to resume cooking.

Step 10: After the cooking time has elapsed, remove the patties from the air fryer.

Step 11: Arrange a lettuce leaf between each burger bun and top with 1 patty.

Step 12: Serve immediately.

Smoky Beef Burgerss

Prep. Time
15 minutes

Cook. Time
10 minutes

Yield
4 Servings

Melt-in-mouth beef burgers with delicious flavours… These beef patties are perfectly seasoned with a dose of deliciousness. The combination of Worcestershire sauce, Maggi seasoning sauce, liquid smoke, and seasoning is the base of burgers' flavouring.

Energy value 220 Kcal I Protein 34.7g
Carbohydrates 1.8g I Fats 7.1g

Ingredients:

- 455g ground beef
- 15ml Worcestershire sauce
- 5g Maggi seasoning sauce
- 3–4 drops liquid smoke
- 1.5g dried parsley
- 2.5g garlic powder
- Salt and ground black pepper, as required
- Non-stick cooking spray

Instructions:

Step 1: In a large bowl, mix together the beef, sauces, liquid smoke, parsley, and spices.

Step 2: Make 4 equal-sized patties from the mixture.

Step 3: Grease the air fryer pan with cooking spray, then slide it inside.

Step 4: Adjust the temperature to 175 °C to preheat for 5 minutes and press the "Start/Pause" button to start preheating.

Step 5: After preheating, place the patties into the preheated air fryer pan in a single layer.

Step 6: With your thumb, make an indent in the centre of each patty and spray with cooking spray.

Step 7: Slide the basket inside and set the timer for 10 minutes.

Step 8: Press the "Start/Pause" button to start cooking.

Step 9: After the cooking time has elapsed, remove the patties from the air fryer and serve hot.

Serving Suggestion: Serve these patties with yoghurt sauce.

Cheesy Beef Meatballs

Prep. Time
15 minutes

Cook. Time
17 minutes

Yield
4 Servings

A super-moist, juicy, and delicious batch of meatballs for your dining table… These meatballs are loaded with ground beef, eggs, breadcrumbs, seasoning, and Parmesan cheese. This easy lunch recipe of cheesy meatballs will be a hit with your family!

Energy value 254 Kcal | Protein 18.2g
Carbohydrates 15.1g | Fats 13.3g

Ingredients:

- 455g ground beef
- 75g breadcrumbs
- 20g Parmesan cheese, grated
- 2 large eggs
- 10g fresh parsley, chopped
- 1 small garlic clove, chopped
- 5g dried oregano, crushed
- Salt and ground black pepper, as required
- Non-stick cooking spray

Instructions:

Step 1: Add all the ingredients in a bowl, and with your hands, mix until well combined.

Step 2: Gently shape the mixture into 2-inch balls.

Step 3: Line the air fryer basket with parchment paper, then grease it with cooking spray.

Step 4: Slide the air fryer basket inside and adjust the temperature to 175 °C to preheat for 5 minutes.

Step 5: Press the "Start/Pause" button to start preheating.

Step 6: After preheating, place the meatballs into the preheated air fryer basket in a single layer.

Step 7: Slide the basket inside and set the timer for 17 minutes.

Step 8: Press the "Start/Pause" button to start cooking.

Step 9: After 11 minutes of cooking, press the "Start/Pause" button to pause cooking.

Step 10: Flip the meatballs and press the "Start/Pause" button to resume cooking.

Step 11: After the cooking time has elapsed, remove the meatballs from the air fryer and serve warm.

Serving Suggestion: Serve these meatballs alongside fresh veggie salad.

Pork Recipes

Hello! Please scan the QR code below to access your promised bonus of all our recipes with full colored photos & beautiful designs! It is the best we could do to keep the book as cheap as possible while providing the best value!

Also, once downloaded you can take the PDF with you digitally wherever you go- meaning you can cook these recipes wherever an Air Fryer is present!

STEP BY STEP Guide To Access-

1) Open Your Phones (Or Any Device You Want The Book On) Back Camera. The Back Camera Is The One You use as if you are taking a picture of someone.

2) Simply point your Camera at the QR code and 'tap' the QR code with your finger to focus the camera.

3) A link / pop up will appear. Simply tap that (and make sure you have internet connection) and the FREE PDF containing all of the colored images should appear.

4) If You Click On The File And It Says 'The File Is Too Big To Preview' Simply click 'Download' and it will download the full book onto your phone!

5) Now you have access to these FOREVER. Simply 'Bookmark' The tab it opened on, or download the document and take wherever you want.

6) Repeat this on any device you want it on!

Any Issues / Feedback / Troubleshooting please email: anthonypublishing123@gmail.com and our customer service team will help you! We want to make sure you have the BEST experience with our books!

Glazed Pork Shoulder

Prep. Time
10 minutes

Cooking Time
18 minutes

Yield
5 Servings

Looking for a divine and flavourful recipe to satisfy your meat cravings? Then try this recipe when you need a delicious meal for family or guests… The glaze of honey, sugar, and soy sauce complements the succulent pork shoulder. Dinner will be ready in a snap!

Energy value 507 Kcal | Protein 31.7g
Carbohydrates 9.7g | Fats 36.9g

Ingredients:

- 90ml soy sauce
- 15g honey
- 5g white sugar
- 910g pork shoulder, cut into 3.75cm thick slices
- Non-stick cooking spray

Instructions:

Step 1: In a large bowl, mix together the soy sauce, sugar, and honey.

Step 2: Add the pork slices and coat with the marinade generously.

Step 3: Cover the bowl and refrigerate to marinate for about 4–6 hours.

Step 4: Grease the air fryer basket with cooking spray, then slide it inside.

Step 5: Adjust the temperature to 175 °C to preheat for 5 minutes and press the "Start/Pause" button to start preheating.

Step 6: After preheating, place the pork slices into the preheated air fryer basket.

Step 7: Slide the basket inside and set the timer for 10 minutes.

Step 8: Press the "Start/Pause" button to start cooking.

Step 9: After 10 minutes of cooking, set the temperature of the air fryer to 200 °C for 8 minutes.

Step 10: After the cooking time has elapsed, remove the pork slices from the air fryer and serve hot.

Serving Suggestion: Serve alongside broccoli mash.

Parsley Pork Loin

Prep. Time
10 minutes

Cooking Time
25 minutes

Yield
6 Servings

A delicious and lavish roasted pork loin recipe… This air fryer recipe is great for the holiday dinner table. You will be a pro at any dinner party where you serve this dish of pork loin.

Energy value 263 Kcal | Protein 29g
Carbohydrates 1.7g | Fats 29g

Ingredients:

- 910g pork loin
- 30ml olive oil
- 2g fresh parsley, chopped
- 2.5g garlic powder
- 2.5g red pepper flakes, crushed
- Salt and ground black pepper, as required
- Non-stick cooking spray

Instructions:

Step 1: Grease the air fryer basket with cooking spray, then slide it inside.

Step 2: Adjust the temperature to 160 °C to preheat for 5 minutes and press the "Start/Pause" button to start preheating.

Step 3: Coat the pork loin with oil, then season evenly with parsley, salt, and black pepper.

Step 4: After preheating, place the pork loin into the preheated air fryer basket.

Step 5: Slide the basket inside and set the timer for 25 minutes.

Step 6: Press the "Start/Pause" button to start cooking.

Step 7: After the cooking time has elapsed, remove the pork loin from the air fryer and place onto a platter for about 5–10 minutes before slicing.

Step 8: Cut the pork loin into slices of the desired size and serve.

Serving Suggestion: Serve with spicy cauliflower.

Glazed Pork Tenderloin

Prep. Time
10 minutes

Cooking Time
25 minutes

Yield
3 Servings

A wonderfully delicious roasted pork tenderloin with perfect texture… This glaze of honey and sriracha adds an aromatic flavouring to the pork tenderloin. This sweet and spicy glaze also enhances the taste of the succulent cut of pork.

Energy value 263 Kcal | Protein 39.7g
Carbohydrates 11.7g | Fats 5.3g

Ingredients:

- 455g pork tenderloin
- 35g honey
- 30ml sriracha
- Salt, as required
- Non-stick cooking spray

Instructions:

Step 1: Grease the air fryer basket with cooking spray, then slide it inside.

Step 2: Adjust the temperature to 160 ºC to preheat for 5 minutes and press the "Start/Pause" button to start preheating.

Step 3: In a small bowl, add the sriracha, honey, and salt, and mix well.

Step 4: Brush the pork tenderloin with the honey mixture evenly.

Step 5: After preheating, place the pork tenderloin into the preheated air fryer basket.

Step 6: Slide the basket inside and set the timer for 25 minutes.

Step 7: Press the "Start/Pause" button to start cooking.

Step 8: After the cooking time has elapsed, remove the pork tenderloin from the air fryer and place onto a platter for about 10 minutes before slicing.

Step 9: Cut the pork tenderloin into slices of the desired size and serve.

Serving Suggestion: Serve with buttered potatoes.

Stuffed Pork Rolls

Prep. Time
15 minutes

Cooking Time
15 minutes

Yield
4 Servings

The best dish for entertaining on special occasions… The delicious veggie stuffing dresses up the tender pork cutlets. These air-fried pork rolls have a variety of tasty flavours and textures that are just perfect for devouring.

Energy value 245 Kcal | Protein 39.8g
Carbohydrates 2g | Fats 8g

Ingredients:

- 1 green onion, chopped
- 30g sun-dried tomatoes, chopped finely
- 5g fresh parsley, chopped
- Salt and ground black pepper, as required
- 4x150g pork cutlets, pounded slightly
- 10g paprika
- 10ml olive oil
- Non-stick cooking spray

Instructions:

Step 1: In a bowl, mix together the green onion, tomatoes, parsley, salt, and black pepper.

Step 2: Spread the tomato mixture over each pork cutlet.

Step 3: Roll each cutlet and secure with cocktail sticks.

Step 4: Rub the outer part of rolls with paprika, salt, and black pepper.

Step 5: Coat the rolls with oil evenly.

Step 6: Grease the air fryer basket with cooking spray, then slide it inside.

Step 7: Adjust the temperature to 200 ºC to preheat for 5 minutes and press the "Start/Pause" button to start preheating.

Step 8: After preheating, place the pork rolls into the preheated air fryer basket.

Step 9: Slide the basket inside and set the timer for 10 minutes.

Step 10: Press the "Start/Pause" button to start cooking.

Step 11: After the cooking time has elapsed, remove the pork rolls from the air fryer and serve hot.

Serving Suggestion: Serve alongside sautéed spinach.

BBQ Pork Ribs

Prep. Time
15 minutes

Cooking Time
15 minutes

Yield
4 Servings

One of the best recipes for making perfect and flavourful pork ribs for your BBQ party… These pork ribs are flavoured with a wonderful marinade of honey, BBQ sauce, ketchup, Worcestershire sauce, soy sauce, and garlic powder.

Energy value 515 Kcal | Protein 32.6g
Carbohydrates 17.9g | Fats 17.8g

Ingredients:

- 55g honey, divided
- 180g BBQ sauce
- 30g tomato ketchup
- 15ml Worcestershire sauce
- 15ml soy sauce
- 2.5g garlic powder
- Ground white pepper, as required
- 800g pork ribs
- Non-stick cooking spray

Instructions:

Step 1: In a large bowl, add all the ingredients except for pork ribs and mix well.

Step 2: Add the pork ribs and coat with the sauce mixture generously.

Step 3: Refrigerate to marinate for about 20 minutes.

Step 4: Grease the air fryer basket with cooking spray, then slide it inside.

Step 5: Adjust the temperature of the air fryer to 180 °C to preheat for 5 minutes and press the "Start/Pause" button to start preheating.

Step 6: After preheating, place the ribs into the preheated air fryer basket.

Step 7: Slide the basket inside and set the timer for 15 minutes.

Step 8: Press the "Start/Pause" button to start cooking.

Step 9: After the cooking time has elapsed, remove the ribs from the air fryer and serve hot.

Serving Suggestion: Serve alongside fresh green salad.

Breaded Pork Chops

Prep. Time
15 minutes

Cooking Time
15 minutes

Yield
2 Servings

A healthy dinner recipe that is also very versatile… With just a handful of ingredients, these crispy chops are really easy to make in your air fryer! The combo of flour and breadcrumbs makes a nicely textured crust for pork chops.

Energy value 567 Kcal | Protein 38.8g
Carbohydrates 54.7g | Fats 22g

Ingredients:

- 2x150g pork chops
- 30g plain flour
- 100g breadcrumbs
- 15ml vegetable oil
- Salt and ground black pepper, as required
- 1 egg
- Non-stick cooking spray

Instructions:

Step 1: Season each pork chop evenly with salt and pepper.

Step 2: Place the flour in a shallow bowl.

Step 3: Crack the egg in a second bowl and beat well.

Step 4: Add the breadcrumbs and oil in a third bowl, and mix until a crumbly mixture forms.

Step 5: Coat the pork chops with flour and dip into the beaten egg. Then coat with the breadcrumbs mixture.

Step 6: Grease the air fryer basket with cooking spray, then slide it inside.

Step 7: Adjust the temperature to 200 °C to preheat for 5 minutes and press the "Start/Pause" button to start preheating.

Step 8: After preheating, place the chops into the preheated air fryer basket in a single layer.

Step 9: Slide the basket inside and set the timer for 15 minutes.

Step 10: Press the "Start/Pause" button to start cooking.

Step 11: After 8 minutes of cooking, press the "Start/Pause" button to pause cooking.

Step 12: Flip the chops and press the "Start/Pause" button to resume cooking.

Step 13: After the cooking time has elapsed, remove the chops from the air fryer and serve hot.

Serving Suggestion: Serve these chops with garlicky green beans.

BBQ Pork Chops

Prep. Time
10 minutes

Cooking Time
16 minutes

Yield
6 Servings

Do you want to enjoy a plate of mouthwatering pork chops in a different style? So try this air fryer recipe to have a good result! This recipe will help you to enjoy one of the best and most richly delicious pork chops at dinner time. BBQ sauce adds an irresistible tasty touch to pork chops.

Energy value 346 Kcal | Protein 38.4g
Carbohydrates 8.3g | Fats 15.9g

Ingredients:

- 6x225g pork loin chops
- Salt and ground black pepper, as required
- 115g BBQ sauce
- Non-stick cooking spray

Instructions:

Step 1: With a meat mallet, pound the chops completely.

Step 2: Sprinkle the chops with a little salt and black pepper.

Step 3: In a large bowl, add the BBQ sauce and chops and mix well.

Step 4: Refrigerate, covered for about 6–8 hours.

Step 5: Remove the chops from the bowl and discard the excess sauce.

Step 6: Grease the air fryer basket with cooking spray, then slide it inside.

Step 7: Adjust the temperature to 180 °C to preheat for 5 minutes and press the "Start/Pause" button to start preheating.

Step 8: After preheating, place the chops into the preheated air fryer basket in a single layer.

Step 9: Slide the basket inside and set the timer for 16 minutes.

Step 10: Press the "Start/Pause" button to start cooking.

Step 11: After 8 minutes of cooking, press the "Start/Pause" button to pause cooking.

Step 12: Flip the chops and press the "Start/Pause" button to resume cooking.

Step 13: After the cooking time has elapsed, remove the chops from the air fryer and serve hot.

Serving Suggestion: Serve these chops alongside sautéed courgette.

Seasoned Pork Chops

Prep. Time
10 minutes

Cooking Time
12 minutes

Yield
4 Servings

A recipe of flavourful pork chops without any fuss… This quick dinner is at your fingertips and comprises succulent, juicy, and tender pork chops with a hint of seasoning. Surely everyone will love these chops.

Energy value 262 Kcal | Protein 39.3g
Carbohydrates 2.2g | Fats 8.8g

Ingredients:

- 4x150g boneless pork chops
- 20g pork rub
- 15ml olive oil
- Non-stick cooking spray

Instructions:

Step 1: Coat both sides of the pork chops with the oil, then rub with the pork rub.

Step 2: Grease the air fryer basket with cooking spray, then slide it inside.

Step 3: Adjust the temperature to 200 °C to preheat for 5 minutes and press the "Start/Pause" button to start preheating.

Step 4: After preheating, place the chops into the preheated air fryer basket in a single layer.

Step 5: Slide the basket inside and set the timer for 12 minutes.

Step 6: Press the "Start/Pause" button to start cooking.

Step 7: After 6 minutes of cooking, press the "Start/Pause" button to pause cooking.

Step 8: Flip the chops and press the "Start/Pause" button to resume cooking.

Step 9: After the cooking time has elapsed, remove the chops from the air fryer and serve hot.

Serving Suggestion: Serve these chops alongside glazed Brussels sprout.

Glazed Ham

Prep. Time
10 minutes

Cooking Time
40 minutes

Yield
4 Servings

A recipe of flavourful pork chops without any fuss… This quick dinner is at your fingertips and comprises succulent, juicy, and tender pork chops with a hint of seasoning. Surely everyone will love these chops.

Energy value 515 Kcal | Protein 32.6g
Carbohydrates 17.9g | Fats 17.8g

Ingredients:

• 750g ham
• 240g whisky
• 30g French mustard
• 25g honey

Instructions:

Step 1: Place the ham at room temperature for about 30 minutes before cooking.

Step 2: In a bowl, mix together the whisky, mustard, and honey.

Step 3: Place the ham in a baking dish and coat the top with half of the honey mixture.

Step 4: Slide the air fryer basket inside and adjust the temperature to 160 ℃ to preheat for 5 minutes.

Step 5: Press the "Start/Pause" button to start preheating.

Step 6: After preheating, place the baking dish into the preheated air fryer basket.

Step 7: Slide the basket inside and set the timer for 40 minutes.

Step 8: Press the "Start/Pause" button to start cooking.

Step 9: After 15 minutes of cooking, press the "Start/Pause" button to pause cooking.

Step 10: Flip the side of the ham and top with the remaining honey mixture.

Step 11: Again, press the "Start/Pause" button to resume cooking.

Step 12: After the cooking time has elapsed, remove the baking dish from the air fryer and place the ham onto a platter for about 10 minutes before slicing.

Step 13: Cut the ham into slices of the desired size and serve.

Serving Suggestion: Serve with orange slices.

Pork Sausage Pizza

Prep. Time
15 minutes

Cooking Time
8 minutes

Yield
1 Servings

Are you ready to prepare a restaurant-quality pizza at home? This air fryer recipe is a great option for you to make a wonderful pizza at home without any fuss… This pizza is an ideal choice for lunch and get-togethers.

Energy value 553 Kcal | Protein 24.4g
Carbohydrates 39.2g | Fats 32.8g

Ingredients:

• 1 pitta bread
• 20g pizza sauce
• 4 pepperoni slices
• 1 cooked pork sausage, sliced
• 2 jalapeño peppers, sliced
• 10g onion, sliced thinly
• 30g mozzarella cheese, grated
• Pinch of dried thyme
• 5ml extra-virgin olive oil

Instructions:

Step 1: Place the pitta bread onto a plate and drizzle with pizza sauce evenly.

Step 2: Arrange the pepperoni slices on top, followed by sausage slices, olives, and onion.

Step 3: Sprinkle with the cheese and thyme, then drizzle with oil.

Step 4: Grease the air fryer basket with cooking spray, then slide it inside.

Step 5: Adjust the temperature to 175 ℃ to preheat for 5 minutes and press the "Start/Pause" button to start preheating.

Step 6: After preheating, place the pizza into the preheated air fryer basket.

Step 7: Slide the basket inside and set the timer for 8 minutes.

Step 8: Press the "Start/Pause" button to start cooking.

Step 9: After the cooking time has elapsed, remove the pizza from the air fryer and transfer onto a serving plate.

Step 10: Set aside to cool slightly before serving.

Lamb Recipes

Hello! Please scan the QR code below to access your promised bonus of all our recipes with full colored photos & beautiful designs! It is the best we could do to keep the book as cheap as possible while providing the best value!

Also, once downloaded you can take the PDF with you digitally wherever you go- meaning you can cook these recipes wherever an Air Fryer is present!

STEP BY STEP Guide To Access-

1) Open Your Phones (Or Any Device You Want The Book On) Back Camera. The Back Camera Is The One You use as if you are taking a picture of someone.

2) Simply point your Camera at the QR code and 'tap' the QR code with your finger to focus the camera.

3) A link / pop up will appear. Simply tap that (and make sure you have internet connection) and the FREE PDF containing all of the colored images should appear.

4) If You Click On The File And It Says 'The File Is Too Big To Preview' Simply click 'Download' and it will download the full book onto your phone!

5) Now you have access to these FOREVER. Simply 'Bookmark' The tab it opened on, or download the document and take wherever you want.

6) Repeat this on any device you want it on!

Any Issues / Feedback / Troubleshooting please email: anthonypublishing123@gmail.com and our customer service team will help you! We want to make sure you have the BEST experience with our books!

Herbed Leg of Lamb

Prep. Time
10 minutes

Cooking Time
1¼ hours

Yield
5 Servings

One of the best dishes for weeknight dinners… This roasted leg of lamb will be also a great hit for a Christmas party. Air fryer cooking gives the leg of lamb a wonderful flavour.

Energy value 468 Kcal | Protein 32.2g
Carbohydrates 0.7g | Fats 36.2g

Ingredients:

- 910g bone-in leg of lamb
- 30ml olive oil
- Salt and ground black pepper, as required
- 2 fresh thyme sprigs
- 1 fresh rosemary sprig
- 1 fresh parsley sprig
- Non-stick cooking spray

Instructions:

Step 1: Coat the leg of lamb with oil and sprinkle with salt and black pepper.

Step 2: Wrap the leg of lamb with the herb sprigs.

Step 3: Grease the air fryer basket with cooking spray, then slide it inside.

Step 4: Adjust the temperature to 150 °C to preheat for 5 minutes and press the "Start/Pause" button to start preheating.

Step 5: After preheating, place the leg of lamb into the preheated air fryer basket.

Step 6: Slide the basket inside and set the timer for 75 minutes.

Step 7: Press the "Start/Pause" button to start cooking.

Step 8: After the cooking time has elapsed, remove the leg of lamb from the air fryer and transfer onto a platter.

Step 9: With a piece of foil, cover the leg of lamb for about 10 minutes before slicing.

Step 10: Cut the leg of lamb into pieces of the desired size and serve.

Serving Suggestion: Serve with roasted potatoes.

Garlicky Lamb Roast

Prep. Time
15 minutes

Cooking Time
1½ hours

Yield
7 Servings

A gorgeous dish of lamb roast for special dinners… You can prepare this succulent and scrumptious lamb roast in an air fryer without any fuss! This lamb roast is flavoured with oil, garlic, rosemary, and simple seasoning.

Energy value 406 Kcal | Protein 50.8g
Carbohydrates 1.4g | Fats 20.7g

Ingredients:

- 1.25kg lamb leg roast
- 3 garlic cloves, cut into thin slices
- 30ml extra-virgin olive oil
- 10g dried rosemary, crushed
- Salt and ground black pepper, as required
- Non-stick cooking spray

Instructions:

Step 1: In a small bowl, mix together the oil, rosemary, salt, and black pepper.

Step 2: With the tip of a sharp knife, make deep slits on the top of the lamb roast's fat.

Step 3: Insert the garlic slices into the slits.

Step 4: Coat the lamb roast evenly with the oil mixture.

Step 5: Grease the air fryer basket with cooking spray, then slide it inside.

Step 6: Adjust the temperature to 190 °C to preheat for 5 minutes and press the "Start/Pause" button to start preheating.

Step 7: After preheating, place the lamb roast into the preheated air fryer basket.

Step 8: Slide the basket inside and set the timer for 15 minutes.

Step 9: Press the "Start/Pause" button to start cooking.

Step 10: After 15 minutes of cooking, immediately adjust the temperature to 160 °C for 75 minutes.

Step 12: After the cooking time has elapsed, remove the lamb roast from the air fryer and transfer onto a platter.

Step 13: With a piece of foil, cover the lamb roast for about 10 minutes before slicing.

Step 14: Cut the leg of lamb into pieces of the desired size and serve.

Serving Suggestion: Serve with roasted sweet potato.

Spiced Lamb Steaks

Prep. Time
15 minutes

Cooking Time
15 minutes

Yield
3 Servings

A hearty lamb steaks recipe with warm spices… With this simple recipe, you can cook amazingly tasty lamb steaks and impress your guests. This recipe is a great choice for dinner with family and friends.

Energy value 368 Kcal I Protein 48.9g
Carbohydrates 4.2g I Fats 17.9g

Ingredients:

- ½ of onion, roughly chopped
- 5g ground fennel
- 2.5g ground cinnamon
- Salt and ground black pepper, as required
- 5 garlic cloves, peeled
- 3g fresh ginger, peeled
- 2.5g ground cumin
- 2.5g cayenne powder
- 680g boneless lamb sirloin steaks

Instructions:

Step 1: In a blender, add the onion, garlic, ginger, and spices, and pulse until smooth.

Step 2: Transfer the mixture into a large bowl.

Step 3: Add the lamb steaks and coat with the mixture generously.

Step 4: Refrigerate to marinate for about 24 hours.

Step 5: Grease the air fryer basket with cooking spray, then slide it inside.

Step 6: Adjust the temperature of the air fryer to 165 °C to preheat for 5 minutes and press the "Start/Pause" button to start preheating.

Step 7: After preheating, place the lamb steaks into the preheated air fryer basket.

Step 8: Slide the basket inside and set the timer for 15 minutes.

Step 9: Press the "Start/Pause" button to start cooking.

Step 10: After 8 minutes of cooking, press the "Start/Pause" button to pause cooking.

Step 11: Flip the steaks and press the "Start/Pause" button to resume cooking.

Step 12: After the cooking time has elapsed, remove the lamb steaks from the air fryer and serve hot.

Serving Suggestion: Serve alongside buttered green peas.

Pesto Rack of Lamb

Prep. Time
15 minutes

Cooking Time
20 minutes

Yield
4 Servings

A rack of lamb recipe with pesto that is just right for a lavish dinner… This recipe proves that you only need the staple ingredients to create a deliciously gourmet Italian-style rack of lamb. This rich pesto is a perfect finish for a delicious rack of lamb.

Energy value 406 Kcal I Protein 34.9g
Carbohydrates 2.9g I Fats 27.7g

Ingredients:

- ½ of bunch fresh mint
- 60ml extra-virgin olive oil
- Salt and ground black pepper, as required
- 1 garlic clove, peeled
- 10g honey
- 1 rack of lamb (680g)

Instructions:

Step 1: For the pesto, in a blender, add the mint, garlic, oil, honey, salt, and black pepper; pulse until smooth.

Step 2: Coat the rack of lamb evenly with some pesto.

Step 3: Grease the air fryer basket with cooking spray, then slide it inside.

Step 4: Adjust the temperature to 95 °C to preheat for 5 minutes and press the "Start/Pause" button to start preheating.

Step 5: After preheating, place the rack of lamb into the preheated air fryer basket.

Step 6: Slide the basket inside and set the timer for 15–20 minutes.

Step 7: Press the "Start/Pause" button to start cooking.

Step 8: While cooking, coat with the remaining pesto after every 5 minutes.

Step 9: After the cooking time has elapsed, remove the rack of lamb from the air fryer and place onto a chopping board for about 5 minutes.

Step 10: Cut the rack into individual chops and serve.

Serving Suggestion: Serve alongside caramelised carrots.

Almond Crusted Rack of Lamb

Prep. Time
15 minutes

Cooking Time
35 minutes

Yield
5 Servings

A lavish meal of rack of lamb for dinner parties… Almonds and breadcrumbs give this rack of lamb a delicious nutty and crispy texture. This elegant dinner meal of nutty-textured rack of lamb comes together in just a few steps.

Energy value 410 Kcal | Protein 37.2g
Carbohydrates 5.4g | Fats 26.3g

Ingredients:

- 15ml olive oil
- 1 garlic clove, minced
- Salt and ground black pepper, as required
- 1 rack of lamb (790g)
- 1 egg
- 10g breadcrumbs
- 85g almonds, finely chopped
- Non-stick cooking spray

Instructions:

Step 1: In a bowl, mix together the oil, garlic, salt, and black pepper.

Step 2: Coat the rack of lamb evenly with oil mixture.

Step 3: Crack the egg in a shallow bowl and beat well.

Step 4: In another bowl, mix together the breadcrumbs and almonds.

Step 5: Dip the rack of lamb in the beaten egg, then coat with the almond mixture.

Step 6: Grease the air fryer basket with cooking spray, then slide it inside.

Step 7: Adjust the temperature to 105 °C to preheat for 5 minutes and press the "Start/Pause" button to start preheating.

Step 8: After preheating, place the rack of lamb into the preheated air fryer basket.

Step 9: Slide the basket inside and set the timer for 30 minutes.

Step 10: Press the "Start/Pause" button to start cooking.

Step 11: After 30 minutes of cooking, adjust the temperature to 200 °C for 5 minutes.

Step 12: After the cooking time has elapsed, remove the rack of lamb from the air fryer and place onto a chopping board for about 5 minutes.

Step 13: Cut the rack into individual chops and serve.

Serving Suggestion: Serve with roasted cauliflower.

Herbed Lamb Chops

Prep. Time
10 minutes

Cooking Time
8 minutes

Yield
2 Servings

A quick recipe of lamb chops with a scrumptious sensation of fresh herbs… These lamb chops are perfectly marinated with herbs and spices, then cooked in the air fryer to perfection.

Energy value 251 Kcal | Protein 32.5g
Carbohydrates 1.1g | Fats 12.3g

Ingredients:

- 15ml fresh lemon juice
- 15ml olive oil
- 1.5g dried rosemary
- 1.5g dried thyme
- 2.5g ground coriander
- 2.5g ground cumin
- Salt and ground black pepper, as required
- 4x115g lamb chops
- Non-stick cooking spray

Instructions:

Step 1: In a large bowl, mix together the lemon juice, oil, herbs, and spices.

Step 2: Add the chops and coat with the herb mixture evenly.

Step 3: Refrigerate to marinate for about 1 hour.

Step 4: Grease the air fryer basket with cooking spray, then slide it inside.

Step 5: Adjust the temperature of the air fryer to 200 °C to preheat for 5 minutes and press the "Start/Pause" button to start preheating.

Step 6: After preheating, place the chops into the preheated air fryer basket in a single layer.

Step 7: Slide the basket inside and set the timer for 7–8 minutes.

Step 8: Press the "Start/Pause" button to start cooking.

Step 9: After 4 minutes of cooking, press the "Start/Pause" button to pause cooking.

Step 10: Flip the chops and press the "Start/Pause" button to resume cooking.

Step 11: After the cooking time has elapsed, remove the chops from the air fryer and serve hot.

Serving Suggestion: Serve with pomegranate and apple salad.

Spiced Lamb Chop

Prep. Time
10 minutes

Cooking Time
9 minutes

Yield
4 Servings

If you are a fan of lamb chops, this is your go-to recipe. Entertain your family with these satisfying spiced lamb chops… These delicious lamb chops are infused with the taste of spices, vinegar, and olive oil.

Energy value 348 Kcal | Protein 42.4g
Carbohydrates 1.3g | Fats 18.4g

Ingredients:

- 30ml olive oil
- 15ml red wine vinegar
- 2.5g ground cumin
- 1.25g garlic powder
- 1.25g onion powder
- 2.25g paprika
- 1.25g cayenne powder
- Salt and ground black pepper, as required
- 4x150g lamb loin chops, trimmed
- Non-stick cooking spray

Instructions:

Step 1: In a large bowl, mix together the oil, vinegar, spices, salt, and black pepper.

Step 2: Add the chops and coat with the spice mixture generously.

Step 3: Refrigerate to marinate for about 1 hour.

Step 4: Remove the chops from the refrigerator and set aside at room temperature for about 15 minutes before cooking.

Step 5: Grease the air fryer basket with cooking spray, then slide it inside.

Step 6: Adjust the temperature of the air fryer to 205 °C to preheat for 5 minutes and press the "Start/Pause" button to start preheating.

Step 7: After preheating, place the chops into the preheated air fryer basket in a single layer.

Step 8: Slide the basket inside and set the timer for 9 minutes.

Step 9: Press the "Start/Pause" button to start cooking.

Step 10: After 5 minutes of cooking, press the "Start/Pause" button to pause cooking.

Step 11: Flip the chops and press the "Start/Pause" button to resume cooking.

Step 12: After the cooking time has elapsed, remove the chops from the air fryer and serve hot.

Serving Suggestion: Serve with couscous salad.

Parsley Lamb Meatballs

Prep. Time
15 minutes

Cooking Time
12 minutes

Yield
4 Servings

If you are a fan of lamb chops, this is your go-to recipe. Entertain your A recipe of aromatic lamb meatballs that are filled with flavour… Ground lamb pairs nicely with cheese, parsley, and seasoning. This family-friendly recipe of meatballs will be loved by all.

Energy value 293 Kcal | Protein 36g
Carbohydrates 9.2g | Fats 11.6g

Ingredients:

- 455g ground lamb
- 1 small onion, chopped roughly
- 10g fresh parsley, chopped roughly
- 2 garlic cloves, peeled
- 30g feta cheese, crumbled
- 35g Italian seasoned breadcrumbs
- 1 egg, lightly beaten
- 10ml Worcestershire sauce
- Salt and ground black pepper, as required
- Non-stick cooking spray

Instructions:

Step 1: In a mini food processor, add the onion, parsley, and garlic, and pulse until finely chopped.

Step 2: Transfer the onion mixture into a large bowl.

Step 3: Add the remaining ingredients and mix until well combined.

Step 4: Make equal-sized balls from the mixture.

Step 5: Grease the air fryer basket with cooking spray, then slide it inside.

Step 6: Adjust the temperature of the air fryer to 205 °C to preheat for 5 minutes and press the "Start/Pause" button to start preheating.

Step 7: After preheating, place the meatballs into the preheated air fryer basket.

Step 8: Slide the basket inside and set the timer for 12 minutes.

Step 9: Press the "Start/Pause" button to start cooking.

Step 10: After the cooking time has elapsed, remove the meatballs from the air fryer and serve hot.

Serving Suggestion: Serve alongside braised scallions.

Spiced Lamb Burgers

Prep. Time
15 minutes

Cooking Time
10 minutes

Yield
6 Servings

One of the most delicious recipes of lamb burgers with a tasty touch of spices... These tasty lamb burgers are made with only the best and most natural ingredients. Ground lamb and spices pair nicely with these burgers.

Energy value 289 Kcal | Protein 42.9g
Carbohydrates 1.4g | Fats 11.2g

Ingredients:

- 910g ground lamb
- 5g cayenne powder
- 5g onion powder
- 5g garlic powder
- 1.25g ground cumin
- 1.25g ground coriander
- Salt and ground black pepper, as required
- Non-stick cooking spray

Instructions:

Step 1: In a bowl, add all ingredients and mix until well combined.

Step 2: Make 6 equal-sized patties from the mixture.

Step 3: Grease the air fryer pan with cooking spray, then slide it inside.

Step 4: Adjust the temperature of the air fryer to 180 °C to preheat for 5 minutes and press the "Start/Pause" button to start preheating.

Step 5: After preheating, place the patties into the preheated air fryer pan.

Step 6: Slide the basket inside and set the timer for 10 minutes.

Step 7: Press the "Start/Pause" button to start cooking.

Step 8: After 5 minutes of cooking, press the "Start/Pause" button to pause cooking.

Step 9: Flip the patties and press the "Start/Pause" button to resume cooking.

Step 10: After the cooking time has elapsed, remove the patties from the air fryer and serve hot.

Serving Suggestion: Serve alongside fennel salad.

Lamb Stuffed Bell Peppers

Prep. Time
20 minutes

Cooking Time
26 minutes

Yield
4 Servings

A healthy meal that is perfect for a light summer supper... Stuff the brightly coloured bell peppers with a filling of lamb, rice, cheese, and a flavourful seasoning combo. These bell peppers are packed with perfectly seasoned ground lamb and cheese filling.

Energy value 435 Kcal | Protein 40g
Carbohydrates 33.3g | Fats 16.3g

Ingredients:

- 5ml olive oil
- ½ of medium onion, chopped
- 2 garlic cloves, minced
- 455g lean ground lamb
- 5g dried basil, crushed
- 5g garlic salt
- 2.5g red chilli powder
- Ground black pepper, as required
- 85g cooked rice
- 75g light Mexican cheese, grated and divided
- 225g tomato sauce, divided
- 10ml Worcestershire sauce
- 4 bell peppers, tops removed and seeded
- Non-stick cooking spray

Instructions:

Step 1: In a medium-sized skillet, heat oil over medium heat and sauté the onion and garlic for about 3–5 minutes or until cooked thoroughly. Add the ground lamb, basil, and spices. Cook for about 8–10 minutes.

Step 2: Remove the skillet from the heat and drain off the excess grease from the skillet.

Step 3: Add the rice, half of the cheese, ☐ of the tomato sauce, and Worcestershire sauce, and mix until well combined.

Step 4: Stuff each bell pepper evenly with the lamb mixture.

Step 5: Grease the air fryer basket with cooking spray, then slide it inside. Adjust the temperature of the air fryer to 205 °C to preheat for 5 minutes and press the "Start/Pause" button to start preheating.

Step 6: After preheating, place the bell peppers into the preheated air fryer basket.Slide the basket inside and set the timer for 11 minutes.Press the "Start/Pause" button to start cooking. After 7 minutes of cooking, press the "Start/Pause" button to pause cooking.

Step 7: Top each bell pepper with the remaining tomato sauce and cheese.

Step 8: Again, press the "Start/Pause" button to resume cooking. After the cooking time has elapsed, remove the bell peppers from the air fryer and serve warm.

Fish Recipes

Hello! Please scan the QR code below to access your promised bonus of all our recipes with full colored photos & beautiful designs! It is the best we could do to keep the book as cheap as possible while providing the best value!

Also, once downloaded you can take the PDF with you digitally wherever you go- meaning you can cook these recipes wherever an Air Fryer is present!

STEP BY STEP Guide To Access-

1) Open Your Phones (Or Any Device You Want The Book On) Back Camera. The Back Camera Is The One You use as if you are taking a picture of someone.

2) Simply point your Camera at the QR code and 'tap' the QR code with your finger to focus the camera.

3) A link / pop up will appear. Simply tap that (and make sure you have internet connection) and the FREE PDF containing all of the colored images should appear.

4) If You Click On The File And It Says 'The File Is Too Big To Preview' Simply click 'Download' and it will download the full book onto your phone!

5) Now you have access to these FOREVER. Simply 'Bookmark' The tab it opened on, or download the document and take wherever you want.

6) Repeat this on any device you want it on!

Any Issues / Feedback / Troubleshooting please email: anthonypublishing123@gmail.com and our customer service team will help you! We want to make sure you have the BEST experience with our books!

Simple Salmon

Prep. Time
10 minutes

Cooking Time
10 minutes

Yield
2 Servings

A quick, super-easy, and delicious salmon recipe… Make an easy, healthy, and tasty meal with this air-fried salmon. Surely this recipe will become the family's all-time favourite dish.

Energy value 286 Kcal I Protein 33g
Carbohydrates 0g I Fats 17.6g

Ingredients:

- Non-stick cooking spray
- 2x170g salmon fillets
- 15ml olive oil
- Salt and ground black pepper, as required

Instructions:

Step 1: Season each salmon fillet with salt and black pepper, then coat with the oil.

Step 2: Grease the air fryer basket with cooking spray, then slide it inside.

Step 3: Adjust the temperature of the air fryer to 185 ºC to preheat for 5 minutes and press the "Start/Pause" button to start preheating.

Step 4: After preheating, place the salmon fillets into the preheated air fryer basket.

Step 5: Slide the basket inside and set the timer for 10 minutes.

Step 6: Press the "Start/Pause" button to start cooking.

Step 7: After the cooking time has elapsed, remove the salmon fillets from the air fryer and serve hot.

Serving Suggestion: Serve alongside Hasselback potatoes.

Spicy Salmon

Prep. Time
10 minutes

Cooking Time
11 minutes

Yield
2 Servings

A lip-smacking recipe of the healthiest salmon… You can add more omega-3 richness to your family's diet with healthy salmon. This aromatic and spicy coating gives the salmon a deep and rich flavour.

Energy value 277 Kcal I Protein 33.5g
Carbohydrates 2.5g I Fats 15.4g

Ingredients:

- 5g smoked paprika
- 2.5g cayenne powder
- 2.5g onion powder
- 2.5g garlic powder
- 2.5g ground cumin
- Salt and ground black pepper, as required
- 10ml olive oil
- 2x150g (3.75cm thick) salmon fillets
- Non-stick cooking spray

Instructions:

Step 1: Add the spices into a bowl and mix well.

Step 2: Drizzle the salmon fillets with oil, then rub with the spice mixture.

Step 3: Grease the air fryer basket with cooking spray, then slide it inside.

Step 4: Adjust the temperature to 200 ºC to preheat for 5 minutes and press the "Start/Pause" button to start preheating.

Step 5: After preheating, place the salmon fillets into the preheated air fryer basket in a single layer.

Step 6: Slide the basket inside and set the timer for 9–11 minutes.

Step 7: Press the "Start/Pause" button to start cooking.

Step 8: After the cooking time has elapsed, remove the salmon fillets from the air fryer and serve hot.

Serving Suggestion: Serve alongside roasted asparagus.

Maple Salmon

Prep. Time
10 minutes

Cooking Time
8 minutes

Yield
2 Servings

A delicious way to treat your family and friends with the healthy benefits of salmon… The natural richness of salmon goes nicely with this simple maple glaze. The sweetness of maple pairs nicely with the omega-3-rich salmon.

Energy value 277 Kcal | Protein 33g
Carbohydrates 13.4g | Fats 10.5g

Ingredients:

- 2x150g salmon fillets
- Salt, as required
- 35g maple syrup
- Non-stick cooking spray

Instructions:

Step 1: Sprinkle the salmon fillets evenly with salt, then coat with maple syrup.

Step 2: Grease the air fryer basket with cooking spray, then slide it inside.

Step 3: Adjust the temperature to 180 °C to preheat for 5 minutes and press the "Start/Pause" button to start preheating.

Step 4: After preheating, place the salmon fillets into the preheated air fryer basket in a single layer.

Step 5: Slide the basket inside and set the timer for 8 minutes.

Step 6: Press the "Start/Pause" button to start cooking.

Step 7: After the cooking time has elapsed, remove the salmon fillets from the air fryer and serve hot.

Serving Suggestion: Serve with quinoa salad.

Salmon with Asparagus

Prep. Time
15 minutes

Cooking Time
11 minutes

Yield
2 Servings

An awesome and warming fish recipe that will be a great addition to your dinner menu… A coating of fresh lemon juice, olive oil, fresh herbs, and seasoning intensifies the flavours of the healthy salmon and asparagus. Surely this meal will become a regular dish in your home.

Energy value 314 Kcal | Protein 35.8g
Carbohydrates 5.2g | Fats 17.9g

Ingredients:

- 20ml fresh lemon juice
- 15ml olive oil
- 2g fresh dill, chopped
- 2g fresh parsley, chopped
- Salt and ground black pepper, as required
- 2x170g boneless salmon fillets
- 225g asparagus
- Non-stick cooking spray

Instructions:

Step 1: In a small bowl, add the lemon juice, oil, herbs, salt, and black pepper, and mix well.

Step 2: In a large bowl, mix together the salmon and ¾ of oil mixture.

Step 3: In a second large bowl, add the asparagus and remaining oil mixture and mix well.

Step 4: Grease the air fryer basket with cooking spray, then slide it inside.

Step 5: Adjust the temperature to 205 °C to preheat for 5 minutes and press the "Start/Pause" button to start preheating.

Step 6: After preheating, place the asparagus into the preheated air fryer basket.

Step 7: Slide the basket inside and set the timer for 11 minutes.

Step 8: Press the "Start/Pause" button to start cooking.

Step 9: After 3 minutes of cooking, press the "Start/Pause" button to pause cooking.

Step 10: Place the salmon fillets on top of asparagus and press the "Start/Pause" button to resume cooking.

Step 11: After the cooking time has elapsed, remove the salmon fillets and asparagus from the air fryer and serve hot.

Salmon with Green Beans

Prep. Time
15 minutes

Cooking Time
12 minutes

Yield
4 Servings

One of the most delicious and wonderful dishes for your family dinner… Rustle up this keto- and paleo-friendly salmon recipe to enjoy as a family meal! This dish is a great combination of nutritious salmon and green beans.

Energy value 6296 Kcal I Protein 31.1g
Carbohydrates 7.3g I Fats 16.8g

Ingredients:

For Green Beans:
- 300g frozen green beans
- 15ml olive oil
- Salt, as required

For Salmon:
- 2 garlic cloves, minced
- 5g fresh dill, chopped
- 130ml fresh lemon juice
- 15ml olive oil
- Salt, as required
- 4x150g salmon fillets

Instructions:

Step 1: Grease the air fryer basket with cooking spray, then slide it inside.

Step 2: Adjust the temperature to 190 °C to preheat for 5 minutes and press the "Start/Pause" button to start preheating.

Step 3: In a large bowl, mix together the green beans, oil, and salt.

Step 4: After preheating, place the green beans into the preheated air fryer basket.

Step 5: Slide the basket inside and set the timer for 12 minutes.

Step 6: Press the "Start/Pause" button to start cooking.

Step 7: Meanwhile, for the salmon, in a bowl, mix together the garlic, dill, lemon juice, olive oil, and salt. After 6 minutes of cooking, press the "Start/Pause" to pause cooking.

Step 8: Remove the basket from the air fryer and flip the green beans.

Step 9: Arrange the salmon fillets on top of green beans.

Step 10: Place the garlic mixture on top of each salmon fillet evenly. Again, slide the basket inside and press the "Start/Pause" to resume cooking.

Step 11: After the cooking time has elapsed, remove the salmon fillets and green beans from the air fryer & serve hot.

Salmon with Broccoli

Prep. Time
10 minutes

Cooking Time
12 minutes

Yield
2 Servings

Do you want to try a healthy salmon recipe which doesn't take long to make and is absolutely delicious? Try this meal that is packed with nutritiously rich ingredients… This meal is a great choice for your dining table.

Energy value 373 Kcal I Protein 31.7g
Carbohydrates 10.6g I Fats 31.7g

Ingredients:

- 135g small broccoli florets
- 30ml vegetable oil, divided
- Salt and ground black pepper, as required
- 5g fresh ginger, grated
- 15ml soy sauce
- 5ml rice vinegar
- 5g light brown sugar
- 1.25g cornflour
- 2x150g skin-on salmon fillets
- Non-stick cooking spray

Instructions:

Step 1: In a bowl, mix together the broccoli, 15ml of oil, salt, and black pepper.

Step 2: In another bowl, add the ginger, soy sauce, vinegar, sugar, and cornflour, and mix well.

Step 3: Coat the salmon fillets evenly with the remaining oil, then coat with the ginger mixture.

Step 4: Grease the air fryer basket with cooking spray, then slide it inside.

Step 5: Adjust the temperature to 190 °C to preheat for 5 minutes and press the "Start/Pause" button to start preheating.

Step 6: After preheating, place the broccoli into the preheated air fryer basket.

Step 7: Place the salmon fillets on top of the broccoli, flesh-side down.

Step 8: Slide the basket inside and set the timer for 12 minutes.

Step 9: After the cooking time has elapsed, remove the salmon fillets and broccoli from the air fryer and serve hot.

Ranch Tilapia

Prep. Time
15 minutes

Cooking Time
13 minutes

Yield
4 Servings

Are you in the mood to eat restaurant-style crispy fish at home? Then follow this amazing and easy recipe of crispy tilapia… This crispy tilapia fish is a great choice for an impromptu party or get-together.

Energy value 274 Kcal | Protein 31.1g
Carbohydrates 4.9g | Fats 14.4g

Ingredients:

• 2 eggs
• 25g cornflakes, crushed
• 1 packet dry ranch-style dressing mix (28g)
• 25ml vegetable oil
• 4x150g tilapia fillets
• Non-stick cooking spray

Instructions:

Step 1: In a shallow bowl, beat the eggs.

Step 2: In another bowl, add the cornflakes, ranch dressing, and oil, and mix until a crumbly mixture forms.

Step 3: Dip the tilapia fillets into the egg, then coat with the cornflake mixture.

Step 4: Grease the air fryer basket with cooking spray, then slide it inside.

Step 5: Adjust the temperature to 180 ºC to preheat for 5 minutes and press the "Start/Pause" button to start preheating.

Step 6: After preheating, place the tilapia fillets into the preheated air fryer basket.

Step 7: Slide the basket inside and set the timer for 13 minutes.

Step 8: Press the "Start/Pause" button to start cooking.

Step 9: After the cooking time has elapsed, remove the tilapia fillets from the air fryer and serve hot.

Serving Suggestion: Serve with bean salad.

Seasoned Tilapia

Prep. Time
10 minutes

Cooking Time
12 minutes

Yield
2 Servings

A super-quick and easy recipe of a healthy fish… This tilapia is seasoned deliciously with a few ingredients. The blend of lemon pepper seasoning, garlic powder, onion powder, salt, and black pepper accentuates the taste of the tilapia.

Energy value 137 Kcal | Protein 28.5g
Carbohydrates 3.5g | Fats 1.4g

Ingredients:

• 2.5g lemon pepper seasoning
• 2.5g garlic powder
• 2.5g onion powder
• Salt and ground black pepper, as required
• 2x150g tilapia fillets
• Non-stick cooking spray
• 1 lemon, cut into wedges

Instructions:

Step 1: In a small bowl, mix together the lemon pepper seasoning, garlic powder, onion powder, salt, and black pepper.

Step 2: Rub the tilapia fillets with the seasoning mixture generously.

Step 3: Grease the air fryer basket with cooking spray, then slide it inside.

Step 4: Adjust the temperature to 180 ºC to preheat for 5 minutes and press the "Start/Pause" button to start preheating.

Step 5: After preheating, place the tilapia fillets into the preheated air fryer basket.

Step 6: Slide the basket inside and set the timer for 12 minutes.

Step 7: Press the "Start/Pause" button to start cooking.

Step 8: After the cooking time has elapsed, remove the tilapia fillets from the air fryer and serve hot alongside the lemon wedges.

Serving Suggestion: Serve alongside buttery mashed potatoes.

Glazed Halibut

Prep. Time
15 minutes

Cooking Time
20 minutes

Yield
3 Servings

It's a time to enjoy the deliciously glazed fish at home… Here is a recipe for glazed halibut with a nice texture and impressive flavouring… This tangy and sweet glaze enhances the flavours of halibut in a wonderfully delicious way.

Energy value 291 Kcal | Protein 34.9g
Carbohydrates 17.3g | Fats 3.6g

Ingredients:

- 1 garlic clove, minced
- 1g fresh ginger, grated
- 120ml cooking wine
- 120ml light soy sauce
- 60ml fresh orange juice
- 30ml fresh lime juice
- 50g sugar
- 1.25g red pepper flakes, crushed
- 455g halibut steak
- Non-stick cooking spray

Instructions:

Step 1: In a medium pan, add the garlic, ginger, wine, soy sauce, juices, sugar, and red pepper flakes, and bring to a boil.

Step 2: Cook for about 3–4 minutes, stirring continuously.

Step 3: Remove the pan of marinade from the heat and let it cool.

Step 4: In a small bowl, add half of the marinade and reserve in a refrigerator.

Step 5: In a resealable bag, add the remaining marinade and halibut steak.

Step 6: Seal the bag and shake to coat well.

Step 7: Refrigerate for about 30 minutes.

Step 8: Grease the air fryer basket with cooking spray, then slide it inside. Adjust the temperature to 200 ºC to preheat for 5 minutes and press the "Start/Pause" button to start preheating.

Step 9: After preheating, place the halibut steak into the preheated air fryer basket. Slide the basket inside and set the timer for 11 minutes. Press the "Start/Pause" button to start cooking.

Step 10: After the cooking time has elapsed, remove the halibut steak from the air fryer and place onto a platter.

Step 11: Cut the steak into 3 equal-sized pieces and coat with the remaining glaze. Serve immediately.

Serving Suggestion: Serve with braised mushrooms.

Cajun Catfish

Prep. Time
15 minutes

Cooking Time
14 minutes

Yield
2 Servings

A delicious catfish recipe with extraordinary flavours… This extraordinary flavour and texture of the fish is obtained with a combo of cornmeal polenta, Cajun seasoning, paprika, and garlic powder. This perfectly spiced fish is delicious and healthy.

Energy value 335 Kcal | Protein 27.7g
Carbohydrates 9.6g | Fats 20.3g

Ingredients:

- 20g cornmeal polenta
- 10g Cajun seasoning
- 2.5g paprika
- 2.5g garlic powder
- Salt, as required
- 15ml olive oil
- 2x170g catfish fillets
- Non-stick cooking spray

Instructions:

Step 1: In a bowl, mix together the cornmeal, Cajun seasoning, paprika, garlic powder, and salt.

Step 2: Add the fish fillets and coat evenly with the mixture.

Step 3: Now, coat each fillet with oil.

Step 4: Grease the air fryer basket with cooking spray, then slide it inside.

Step 5: Adjust the temperature to 200 ºC to preheat for 5 minutes and press the "Start/Pause" button to start preheating.

Step 6: After preheating, place the fish fillets into the preheated air fryer basket.

Step 7: Slide the basket inside and set the timer for 12–14 minutes.

Step 8: Press the "Start/Pause" button to start cooking.

Step 9: After 7 minutes of cooking, press the "Start/Pause" button to pause cooking.

Step 10: Flip the fish fillets and press the "Start/Pause" button to resume cooking.

Step 11: After the cooking time has elapsed, remove the fish fillets from the air fryer and serve hot.

Serving Suggestion: Serve with apple salad.potatoes.

Crispy Catfish

Prep. Time
20 minutes

Cooking Time
15 minutes

Yield
5 Servings

An extremely easy way to make a superb-tasting crispy fish… Your family will love this fish so much. This crispy and crunchy air-fried fish will be a new favourite for kids and adults alike.

Energy value 317 Kcal | Protein 27.8g
Carbohydrates 19.6g | Fats 13.9g

Ingredients:

- 5x150g catfish fillets
- 240ml milk
- 10ml fresh lemon juice
- 100g yellow mustard
- 70g cornmeal
- 30g plain flour
- 5g dried parsley flakes
- 1.25g red chilli powder
- 1.25g cayenne powder
- 1.25g onion powder
- 1.25g garlic powder
- Salt and ground black pepper, as required
- Non-stick cooking spray

Instructions:

Step 1: In a large bowl, place the catfish, milk, and lemon juice, and refrigerate for about 15 minutes.

Step 2: In a shallow bowl, place the mustard.

Step 3: In another bowl, mix together the cornmeal, flour, parsley flakes, and spices.

Step 4: Remove the catfish fillets from the milk mixture, and with paper towels, pat them dry.

Step 5: Coat each fish fillet with mustard, then roll into the cornmeal mixture.

Step 6: Grease the air fryer basket with cooking spray, then slide it inside. Adjust the temperature to 200 ºC to preheat for 5 minutes and press the "Start/Pause" button to start preheating.

Step 7: After preheating, place the fish fillets into the preheated air fryer basket and spray with the cooking spray.

Step 8: Slide the basket inside and set the timer for 15 minutes. Press the "Start/Pause" button to start cooking. After 10 minutes of cooking, press the "Start/Pause" button to pause cooking.

Step 9: Flip the fish fillets and spray with the cooking spray. Again, press the "Start/Pause" button to resume cooking.

Step 10: After the cooking time has elapsed, remove the fish fillets from the air fryer and serve hot.

Serving Suggestion: Serve alongside French fries.

Sesame Seed Tuna

Prep. Time
10 minutes

Cooking Time
6 minutes

Yield
2 Servings

A flavourful plate of tuna fillet with sesame seeds… This recipe is a healthy way to prepare tuna for dinner. This deliciously healthy tuna is baked to perfection using the most advanced technology of an air fryer.

Energy value 399 Kcal | Protein 50.2g
Carbohydrates 4.8g | Fats 19.4g

Ingredients:

- 1 egg white
- 25g white sesame seeds
- 10g black sesame seeds
- Salt and ground black pepper, as required
- 2x150g tuna steaks

Instructions:

Step 1: In a bowl, mix together the cornmeal, Cajun seasoning, paprika, garlic powder, and salt.

Step 2: Add the fish fillets and coat evenly with the mixture.

Step 3: Now, coat each fillet with oil.

Step 4: Grease the air fryer basket with cooking spray, then slide it inside.

Step 5: Adjust the temperature to 200 ºC to preheat for 5 minutes and press the "Start/Pause" button to start preheating.

Step 6: After preheating, place the fish fillets into the preheated air fryer basket.

Step 7: Slide the basket inside and set the timer for 12–14 minutes.

Step 8: Press the "Start/Pause" button to start cooking.

Step 9: After 7 minutes of cooking, press the "Start/Pause" button to pause cooking.

Step 10: Flip the fish fillets and press the "Start/Pause" button to resume cooking.

Step 11: After the cooking time has elapsed, remove the fish fillets from the air fryer and serve hot.

Serving Suggestion: Serve with apple salad.potatoes.

Pesto Haddock

Prep. Time
15 minutes

Cooking Time
8 minutes

Yield
2 Servings

A perfect and super-quick weeknight dinner... Here is the best recipe to cook haddock in an air fryer with Italian flair! The coating of pesto enhances the flavour of the haddock with deliciousness.

Energy value 335 Kcal | Protein 27.7g
Carbohydrates 9.6g | Fats 20.3g

Ingredients:

- 2x150g haddock fillets
- 15ml olive oil
- Salt and ground black pepper, as required
- Non-stick cooking spray
- 20g pine nuts
- 10g fresh basil, chopped
- 10g Parmesan cheese, grated
- 90ml extra-virgin olive oil

Instructions:

Step 1: Coat the fish fillets evenly with oil and sprinkle with salt and black pepper.

Step 2: Grease the air fryer basket with cooking spray, then slide it inside.

Step 3: Adjust the temperature to 180 °C to preheat for 5 minutes and press the "Start/Pause" button to start preheating.

Step 4: After preheating, place the fish fillets into the preheated air fryer basket in a single layer.

Step 5: Slide the basket inside and set the timer for 8 minutes.

Step 6: Press the "Start/Pause" button to start cooking.

Step 7: Meanwhile, for the pesto, add the remaining ingredients in a food processor and pulse until smooth.

Step 8: After the cooking time has elapsed, remove the fish fillets from the air fryer and place onto a platter.

Step 9: Top each fish fillet with the pesto and serve.

Serving Suggestion: Serve alongside spiralised veggie salad.

Breaded Flounder

Prep. Time
15 minutes

Cooking Time
12 minutes

Yield
4 Servings

One of the most enjoyable dishes of flounder... There are a few tricks for you to make a fish with extraordinarily crispy goodness. This crispy coating of breadcrumbs greatly enhances the flavour of nutritious flounder.

Energy value 456 Kcal | Protein 40.2g
Carbohydrates 5.4g | Fats 20.2g

Ingredients:

- 1 egg
- 120g dry breadcrumbs
- 60ml vegetable oil
- 4x170g flounder fillets
- Non-stick cooking spray
- 1 lemon, sliced

Instructions:

Step 1: In a shallow bowl, beat the egg.

Step 2: In another bowl, add the breadcrumbs and oil, and mix until crumbly mixture is formed.

Step 3: Dip flounder fillets into the beaten egg, then coat with the breadcrumb mixture.

Step 4: Grease the air fryer basket with cooking spray, then slide it inside.

Step 5: Adjust the temperature to 180 °C to preheat for 5 minutes and press the "Start/Pause" button to start preheating.

Step 6: After preheating, place the flounder fillets into the preheated air fryer basket in a single layer.

Step 7: Slide the basket inside and set the timer for 12 minutes.

Step 8: Press the "Start/Pause" button to start cooking.

Step 9: After the cooking time has elapsed, remove the flounder fillets from the air fryer and serve hot.

Serving Suggestion: Serve with roasted potatoes.

Crispy Cod

Prep. Time
15 minutes

Cooking Time
15 minutes

Yield
4 Servings

A family-friendly fish recipe for weekends…
This recipe of cod is a fine example of
high-quality cooking with an exquisite crispy
taste and tender texture. This flavoursome
crispy coating adds a delicious richness to
the healthy cod.

Energy value 227 Kcal I Protein 25.2g
Carbohydrates 11.7g I Fats 4.7g

Ingredients:

- 4x115g cod fillets
- Salt, as required
- 40g plain flour
- 2 eggs
- 60g panko breadcrumbs
- 2.5g dry mustard
- 2g fresh dill, minced
- 2.5g lemon zest, grated
- 2.5g onion powder
- 2.5g paprika
- Non-stick cooking spray

Instructions:

Step 1: Season the cod fillets with salt generously.

Step 2: In a shallow bowl, place the flour.

Step 3: Crack the eggs in a second bowl and beat well.

Step 4: In a third bowl, mix together the panko, dill, lemon
zest, mustard, and spices.

Step 5: Coat each cod fillet with the flour and dip into the
beaten eggs. Then coat with the panko mixture.

Step 6: Grease the air fryer basket with cooking spray, then
slide it inside.

Step 7: Adjust the temperature to 200 °C to preheat for 5
minutes and press the "Start/Pause" button to start preheating.

Step 8: After preheating, place the cod fillets into the
preheated air fryer basket in a single layer.

Step 9: Slide the basket inside and set the timer for 15
minutes. Press the "Start/Pause" button to start cooking.

Step 10: After 8 minutes of cooking, press the "Start/Pause"
button to pause cooking.

Step 11: Flip the cod fillets and press the "Start/Pause" button
to resume cooking.

Step 12: After the cooking time has elapsed, remove the cod
fillets from the air fryer and serve hot.

Serving Suggestion: Serve with coleslaw.

Seafood Recipes

Hello! Please scan the QR code below to access your promised bonus of all our recipes with full colored photos & beautiful designs! It is the best we could do to keep the book as cheap as possible while providing the best value!

Also, once downloaded you can take the PDF with you digitally wherever you go- meaning you can cook these recipes wherever an Air Fryer is present!

STEP BY STEP Guide To Access-

1) Open Your Phones (Or Any Device You Want The Book On) Back Camera. The Back Camera Is The One You use as if you are taking a picture of someone.

2) Simply point your Camera at the QR code and 'tap' the QR code with your finger to focus the camera.

3) A link / pop up will appear. Simply tap that (and make sure you have internet connection) and the FREE PDF containing all of the colored images should appear.

4) If You Click On The File And It Says 'The File Is Too Big To Preview' Simply click 'Download' and it will download the full book onto your phone!

5) Now you have access to these FOREVER. Simply 'Bookmark' The tab it opened on, or download the document and take wherever you want.

6) Repeat this on any device you want it on!

Any Issues / Feedback / Troubleshooting please email: anthonypublishing123@gmail.com and our customer service team will help you! We want to make sure you have the BEST experience with our books!

Spicy Prawn

Prep. Time
15 minutes

Cooking Time
5 minutes

Yield
2 Servings

A simple recipe that makes prawns delicious and filling… The flavoursome spicy prawn recipe is a truly delicious meal for any time of day. Surely this prawn recipe will become a family favourite.

Energy value 253 Kcal I Protein 35.7g
Carbohydrates 0.7g I Fats 11.5g

Ingredients:

- Non-stick cooking spray
- 340g tiger prawns, peeled and deveined
- 20ml olive oil
- 2.5g Old Bay Seasoning
- 1.25g cayenne powder
- 1.25g smoked paprika
- Salt, as required

Instructions:

Step 1: Grease the air fryer basket with cooking spray, then slide it inside.

Step 2: Adjust the temperature to 200 °C to preheat for 5 minutes and press the "Start/Pause" button to start preheating.

Step 3: In a large bowl, add the prawns, oil, and spices, and mix well.

Step 4: After preheating, place the prawns into the preheated air fryer basket in a single layer.

Step 5: Slide the basket inside and set the timer for 5 minutes.

Step 6: Press the "Start/Pause" button to start cooking.

Step 7: After the cooking time has elapsed, remove the prawns from the air fryer and serve hot.

Serving Suggestion: Serve alongside garlicky green beans.

Prawn Scampi

Prep. Time
15 minutes

Cooking Time
7 minutes

Yield
4 Servings

Do you want a tempting treat of prawns to satisfy your taste buds? This authentic Italian recipe is a wonderfully delicious supper of prawns that is insanely easy to assemble… The prawns are smothered in a super-tasty sauce of wine, lemon juice, garlic, and fresh herbs.

Energy value 221 Kcal I Protein 26.4g
Carbohydrates 3.7g I Fats 10.5g

Ingredients:

- 40g salted butter
- 15ml fresh lemon juice
- 4g garlic, minced
- 10g red pepper flakes, crushed
- 455g prawns, peeled and deveined
- 3g fresh basil, chopped
- 2g fresh chives, chopped
- 15ml dry white wine

Instructions:

Step 1: Place a 7-inch round baking dish in the air fryer pan.

Step 2: Slide the air fryer basket inside and adjust the temperature to 160 °C to preheat for 5 minutes and press the "Start/Pause" button to start preheating.

Step 3: After preheating, place butter, lemon juice, garlic, and red pepper flakes into the heated baking dish and mix well.

Step 4: Slide the pan inside and set the timer for 7 minutes.

Step 5: Press the "Start/Pause" button to start cooking.

Step 6: After 2 minutes of cooking, press the "Start/Pause" button to pause cooking.

Step 7: Add the prawns, basil, chives, and wine into the pan and stir to combine.

Step 8: Again, press the "Start/Pause" button to resume cooking.

Step 9: After the cooking time has elapsed, remove the baking dish from the air fryer and place onto a wire rack for about 1 minute.

Step 10: Stir the prawn mixture and serve hot.

Prawn Kebabs

Prep. Time
10 minutes

Cooking Time
8 minutes

Yield
2 Servings

A recipe of prawn kebabs that is cooked without the outdoor grill… This delicious lunch is super-quick and easy… The juicy prawns are seasoned with the blend of lemon, fresh coriander, and spices, and then cooked in the air fryer.

Energy value 216 Kcal I Protein 39.3g
Carbohydrates 4.5g I Fats 3.5g

Ingredients:

• 340g prawns, peeled and deveined
• 30ml fresh lemon juice
• 2g garlic, minced
• 2g fresh coriander, chopped
• 2.5g ground cumin
• 2.5g paprika
• 2.5g ground cumin
• Salt and ground black pepper, as required
• Non-stick cooking spray

Instructions:

Step 1: In a bowl, mix together the lemon juice, garlic, coriander, and spices.

Step 2: Add the prawns and mix well.

Step 3: Thread the prawns onto pre-soaked wooden skewers.

Step 4: Grease the air fryer basket with cooking spray, then slide inside.

Step 5: Adjust the temperature to 175 °C to preheat for 5 minutes and press the "Start/Pause" button to start preheating.

Step 6: After preheating, place the prawn skewers into the preheated air fryer basket in a single layer.

Step 7: Slide the basket inside and set the timer for 8 minutes.

Step 8: Press the "Start/Pause" button to start cooking.

Step 9: After 4 minutes of cooking, press the "Start/Pause" button to pause cooking.

Step 10: Flip the skewers and press the "Start/Pause" button to resume cooking.

Step 11: After the cooking time has elapsed, remove the prawn skewers from the air fryer and serve.

Serving Suggestion: Serve alongside fresh baby greens.

Prawn Burgers

Prep. Time
15 minutes

Cooking Time
6 minutes

Yield
2 Servings

A batch of prawn burgers with a mild spicy kick… These wonderfully delicious burgers are really enjoyable for a lunch treat. You can complement these delicious prawn burgers with a side of fresh greens and sour cream.

Energy value 208 Kcal I Protein 13.1g
Carbohydrates 31.3g I Fats 3.2g

Ingredients:

• 65g prawns, peeled, deveined, and finely chopped
• 75g breadcrumbs
• 20–25g onion, finely chopped
• 2.5g fresh ginger, minced
• 2.5g garlic, minced
• 2.5g red chilli powder
• 2.5g ground cumin
• 1.25g ground turmeric
• Salt and ground black pepper, as required
• Non-stick cooking spray
• 60g fresh baby spinach

Instructions:

Step 1: In a large bowl, mix together the prawns, breadcrumbs, onion, ginger, garlic, and spices.

Step 2: Make small patties from the mixture.

Step 3: Grease the air fryer basket with cooking spray, then slide inside.

Step 4: Adjust the temperature to 175 °C to preheat for 5 minutes and press the "Start/Pause" button to start preheating.

Step 5: After preheating, place the patties into the preheated air fryer basket in a single layer.

Step 6: Slide the basket inside and set the timer for 5–6 minutes.

Step 7: Press the "Start/Pause" button to start cooking.

Step 8: After the cooking time has elapsed, remove the patties from the air fryer and serve alongside the baby spinach.

Buttered Scallops

Prep. Time
15 minutes

Cooking Time
4 minutes

Yield
2 Servings

A fantastic plate of scallops that is prepared within 20 minutes… The super-tasty scallops are cooked in the air fryer with the use of minimal ingredients. The blending of butter, fresh thyme, and seasoning make the scallops flavourful and moist.

Energy value 206 Kcal | Protein 28.7g
Carbohydrates 4.7g | Fats 7.4g

Ingredients:

- Non-stick cooking spray
- 340g sea scallops, cleaned and patted very dry
- 15g butter, melted
- 2g fresh thyme, minced
- Salt and ground black pepper, as required

Instructions:

Step 1: Grease the air fryer basket with cooking spray, then slide inside.

Step 2: Adjust the temperature to 200 °C to preheat for 5 minutes and press the "Start/Pause" button to start preheating.

Step 3: In a large bowl, add the scallops, butter, thyme, salt, and black pepper. Toss to coat well.

Step 4: After preheating, place the scallops into the preheated air fryer basket in a single layer.

Step 5: Slide the basket inside and set the timer for 4 minutes.

Step 6: Press the "Start/Pause" button to start cooking.

Step 7: After the cooking time has elapsed, remove the scallops from the air fryer and serve.

Scallops with Capers Sauce

Prep. Time
15 minutes

Cooking Time
6 minutes

Yield
2 Servings

Do you want to turn plain scallops into a special meal? Then try this fast and healthy air fryer recipe to cook scallops with a tasty capers sauce… Capers, lemon, parsley, and garlic combine beautifully for this dish.

Energy value 227 Kcal | Protein 19.2g
Carbohydrates 4.1g | Fats 15.1g

Ingredients:

- Non-stick cooking spray
- 8x28g sea scallops, cleaned and patted very dry
- Salt and ground black pepper, as required
- 30ml extra-virgin olive oil
- 5g fresh parsley, finely chopped
- 10g capers, finely chopped
- 5g fresh lemon zest, finely grated
- 5g garlic, finely chopped

Instructions:

Step 1: Grease the air fryer basket with cooking spray, then slide inside.

Step 2: Adjust the temperature to 200 °C to preheat for 5 minutes and press the "Start/Pause" button to start preheating.

Step 3: Season each scallop evenly with salt and black pepper.

Step 4: After preheating, place the scallops into the preheated air fryer basket in a single layer.

Step 5: Slide the basket inside and set the timer for 6 minutes.

Step 6: Press the "Start/Pause" button to start cooking.

Step 7: Meanwhile, for the sauce, mix the remaining ingredients in a bowl.

Step 8: After the cooking time has elapsed, remove the scallops from the air fryer and place onto serving plates.

Step 9: Top with the sauce and serve immediately.

Scallops with Spinach

Prep. Time
15 minutes

Cooking Time
10 minutes

Yield
2 Servings

A spectacular, tasty, and healthy pairing of scallops and spinach... The creamy sauce of tomatoes, basil, and garlic dresses up the scallops and spinach deliciously. Surely this dish will brighten your dining table.

Energy value 203 Kcal | Protein 26.4g
Carbohydrates 12.3g | Fats 18.3g

Ingredients:

- 1 bag frozen spinach, thawed and drained (340g)
- Non-stick cooking spray
- Salt and ground black pepper, as required
- 210ml heavy whipping cream
- 20g tomato paste
- 2g garlic, minced
- 2g fresh basil, chopped
- 8 jumbo sea scallops

Instructions:

Step 1: In the bottom of a heatproof pan, place the spinach.

Step 2: Spray with cooking spray, then sprinkle with a little salt and black pepper.

Step 3: Arrange the scallops on top of the spinach in a single layer.

Step 4: In a bowl, add cream, tomato paste, garlic, basil, salt, and black pepper, and mix well.

Step 5: Place the cream mixture evenly over the spinach and scallops.

Step 6: Slide the air fryer basket inside and adjust the temperature to 175 °C to preheat for 5 minutes.

Step 7: Press the "Start/Pause" button to start preheating.

Step 8: After preheating, place the pan into the preheated air fryer basket.

Step 9: Slide the basket inside and set the timer for 10 minutes.

Step 10: Press the "Start/Pause" button to start cooking.

Step 11: After the cooking time has elapsed, remove the pan from the air fryer and serve hot.

Crab Cakes

Prep. Time
20 minutes

Cooking Time
20 minutes

Yield
2 Servings

A unique but delicious twist on meat burgers... The best crab cakes that are perfect for a party and family gatherings... These crab cakes will spice up your weekly lunch in a healthy and tasty way.

Energy value 213 Kcal | Protein 20.3g
Carbohydrates 7.8g | Fats 15.3g

Ingredients:

- 225g lump crab meat
- 30g panko breadcrumbs
- 25g green onion, finely chopped
- 1 large egg
- 15g mayonnaise
- 2.5g Dijon mustard
- 2.5ml Worcestershire sauce
- 5g Old Bay Seasoning
- Ground black pepper, as required
- Non-stick cooking spray
- 4 lettuce leaves, torn

Instructions:

Step 1: In a large bowl, add all the ingredients, and gently stir to combine.

Step 2: Cover the bowl and refrigerate for about 1 hour.

Step 3: Make 4 equal-sized patties from the mixture.

Step 4: Grease the air fryer basket with cooking spray, then slide inside.

Step 5: Adjust the temperature to 190 °C to preheat for 5 minutes and press the "Start/Pause" button to start preheating.

Step 6: After preheating, place the patties into the preheated air fryer basket in a single layer.

Step 7: Slide the basket inside and set the timer for 10 minutes.

Step 8: Press the "Start/Pause" button to start cooking.

Step 9: After 5 minutes of cooking, press the "Start/Pause" button to pause cooking.

Step 10: Flip the patties and press the "Start/Pause" button to resume cooking.

Step 11: After the cooking time has elapsed, remove the patties from the air fryer and serve alongside the lettuce.

Buttered Crab Shells

Prep. Time
15 minutes

Cooking Time
10 minutes

Yield
4 Servings

An easy crab legs recipe with a crispy topping that's ready in just 25 minutes! This recipe is a delicious and flavourful way to prepare crab shells that seafood lovers will enjoy. Serve these scrumptious buttery crab shells with fresh baby greens.

Energy value 631 Kcal | Protein 48.9g
Carbohydrates 15.6g | Fats 20.1g

Ingredients:

- 4 soft crab shells, cleaned
- 240ml buttermilk
- 3 eggs
- 300g panko breadcrumb
- 10g seafood seasoning
- 2g lemon zest, grated
- 35g butter, melted
- Non-stick cooking spray

Instructions:

Step 1: In a shallow bowl, place the buttermilk.

Step 2: In a second bowl, whisk the eggs.

Step 3: In a third bowl, mix together the breadcrumbs, seafood seasoning, and lemon zest.

Step 4: Soak the crab shells into the buttermilk for about 10 minutes.

Step 5: Now, dip the crab shells into the beaten eggs, then coat with the breadcrumbs mixture.

Step 6: Grease the air fryer basket with cooking spray, then slide it inside.

Step 7: Adjust the temperature of the air fryer to 190 °C to preheat for 5 minutes and press the "Start/Pause" button to start preheating.

Step 8: After preheating, place the crab shells into the preheated air fryer basket.

Step 9: Slide the basket inside and set the timer for 8–10 minutes.

Step 10: Press the "Start/Pause" button to start cooking.

Step 11: After the cooking time has elapsed, remove the crab shells from the air fryer and transfer onto serving plates.

Step 12: Drizzle crab shells with melted butter and serve immediately.

Seafood with Pasta

Prep. Time
15 minutes

Cooking Time
18 minutes

Yield
4 Servings

A very tasty but easy-to-prepare main course meal… Salmon and prawns with tomatoes is seriously one of the most delicious meals you can make with pasta! This dish is a great and tasty choice to impress a crowd.

Energy value 476 Kcal | Protein 37.2g
Carbohydrates 32.4g | Fats 22.7g

Ingredients:

- 395g pasta (of your choice)
- 65g pesto, divided
- 4x115g salmon steaks
- 30ml olive oil
- 225g cherry tomatoes, chopped
- 8 large prawns, peeled and deveined
- 30ml fresh lemon juice
- 5g fresh thyme, chopped

Instructions:

Step 1: In a large pan of the salted boiling water, add the pasta and cook for about 8–10 minutes or until desired doneness.

Step 2: Drain the pasta and transfer into a large bowl. Set aside.

Step 3: Meanwhile, in the bottom of a baking dish, spread a little pesto.

Step 4: Place the salmon steaks and tomatoes over pesto in a single layer and drizzle evenly with the oil.

Step 5: Now, add the prawns on top in a single layer.

Step 6: Drizzle with lemon juice and sprinkle with thyme.

Step 7: Slide the air fryer basket inside and adjust the temperature to 200 °C to preheat for 5 minutes.

Step 8: Press the "Start/Pause" button to start preheating.

Step 9: After preheating, place the baking dish into the preheated air fryer basket.

Step 10: Slide the basket inside and set the timer for 8 minutes.

Step 11: Press the "Start/Pause" button to start cooking.

Step 12: After the cooking time has elapsed, remove the baking dish from the air fryer and stir in the remaining pesto.

Step 13: Divide the pasta onto serving plates and top with the salmon mixture.

Step 14: Serve immediately.

Vegetarian Recipes

Hello! Please scan the QR code below to access your promised bonus of all our recipes with full colored photos & beautiful designs! It is the best we could do to keep the book as cheap as possible while providing the best value!

Also, once downloaded you can take the PDF with you digitally wherever you go- meaning you can cook these recipes wherever an Air Fryer is present!

STEP BY STEP Guide To Access-

1) Open Your Phones (Or Any Device You Want The Book On) Back Camera. The Back Camera Is The One You use as if you are taking a picture of someone.

2) Simply point your Camera at the QR code and 'tap' the QR code with your finger to focus the camera.

3) A link / pop up will appear. Simply tap that (and make sure you have internet connection) and the FREE PDF containing all of the colored images should appear.

4) If You Click On The File And It Says 'The File Is Too Big To Preview' Simply click 'Download' and it will download the full book onto your phone!

5) Now you have access to these FOREVER. Simply 'Bookmark' The tab it opened on, or download the document and take wherever you want.

6) Repeat this on any device you want it on!

Any Issues / Feedback / Troubleshooting please email: anthonypublishing123@gmail.com and our customer service team will help you! We want to make sure you have the BEST experience with our books!

Potato Salad

Prep. Time
15 minutes

Cooking Time
40 minutes

Yield
6 Servings

A nice and delicious potato salad to be packed in your lunchbox… This recipe involves preparing a healthy salad that will also be perfect for your dining table. Air-fried potatoes are blended with a combination of eggs, mayonnaise, celery, onion, mustard, and seasoning.

Energy value 202 Kcal | Protein 5.7g
Carbohydrates 26.8g | Fats 8.5g

Ingredients:

- 4 Russet potatoes
- 15ml olive oil
- Salt, as required
- Non-stick cooking spray
- 3 hard-boiled eggs, peeled and chopped
- 100g celery, chopped
- 60g red onion, chopped
- 20g prepared mustard
- 1.25g celery salt
- 1.25g garlic salt
- 65g mayonnaise

Instructions:

Step 1: With a fork, prick the potatoes.

Step 2: Drizzle with oil and rub with the salt.

Step 3: Grease the air fryer basket with cooking spray, then slide it inside.

Step 4: Adjust the temperature of the air fryer to 200 °C to preheat for 5 minutes and press the "Start/Pause" button to start preheating.

Step 5: After preheating, place the potatoes into the preheated air fryer basket.

Step 6: Slide the basket inside and set the timer for 35–40 minutes.

Step 7: Press the "Start/Pause" button to start cooking.

Step 8: After the cooking time has elapsed, remove the potatoes from the air fryer and transfer into a bowl.

Step 9: Set aside to cool.

Step 10: After cooking, peel the potatoes and chop them.

Step 11: In a salad bowl, add the potatoes and remaining ingredients, and gently stir to combine.

Step 12: Refrigerate to chill before serving.

Courgette Salad

Prep. Time
15 minutes

Cooking Time
15 minutes

Yield
4 Servings

A super-simple salad with veggie flavours, Parmesan cheese, and refreshing lemon juice… This courgette salad is a perfect choice for your lunch. You will find that you love making this veggie salad again and again.

Energy value 134 Kcal | Protein 5.9g
Carbohydrates 10.1g | Fats 5.9g

Ingredients:

- 455g courgettes, cut into rounds
- 30ml olive oil
- 5g garlic powder
- Salt and ground black pepper, as required
- Non-stick cooking spray
- 2 large tomatoes, sliced
- 150g fresh spinach, chopped
- 30g Parmesan cheese, grated
- 30ml fresh lemon juice

Instructions:

Step 1: Grease the air fryer basket with cooking spray, then slide it inside.

Step 2: Adjust the temperature of the air fryer to 90 °C to preheat for 5 minutes and press the "Start/Pause" button to start preheating.

Step 3: In a bowl, mix together the courgette, oil, garlic powder, salt, and black pepper.

Step 4: After preheating, place the courgette slices into the preheated air fryer basket.

Step 5: Slide the basket inside and set the timer for 12–15 minutes.

Step 6: After 8 minutes of cooking, press the "Start/Pause" button to pause cooking.

Step 7: Flip the courgette slices and press the "Start/Pause" button to resume cooking.

Step 8: After the cooking time has elapsed, remove the courgette slices from the air fryer and transfer onto a plate.

Step 9: Set aside to cool.

Step 10: In a salad bowl, add the cooked courgette slices, spinach, tomato, lemon juice, salt, and black pepper, and toss to coat well.

Step 11: Top with Parmesan cheese and serve immediately.

Brussels Sprout Salad

Prep. Time
20 minutes

Cooking Time
15 minutes

Yield
6 Servings

A wonderful combination of nutritiousness and deliciousness… The combination of Brussels sprouts, apples, and dressing makes a unique and magnificent salad for your lunch. This will be a great addition to your salad menu.

Energy value 177 Kcal | Protein 3.4g
Carbohydrates 28.1g | Fats 7.7g

Ingredients:

- Non-stick cooking spray

For Brussels Sprouts:

- 455g medium Brussels sprouts, trimmed and halved vertically
- 15ml olive oil
- Salt and ground black pepper, as required
- 3 apples, cored and chopped
- 1 red onion, sliced
- 375g lettuce, torn

For Dressing:

- 30ml extra-virgin olive oil
- 15ml fresh lemon juice
- 15ml apple cider vinegar
- 15g maple syrup
- 5g Dijon mustard
- Salt and ground black pepper, as required

Instructions:

Step 1: Grease the air fryer basket with cooking spray, then slide it inside. Adjust the temperature of the air fryer to 90 °C to preheat for 5 minutes and press the "Start/Pause" button to start preheating.

Step 2: In a bowl, add the Brussels sprouts, oil, salt, and black pepper, and toss to coat well.

Step 3: After preheating, place the Brussels sprout halves into the preheated air fryer basket. Slide the basket inside and set the timer for 15 minutes.

Step 4: After 8 minutes of cooking, press the "Start/Pause" button to pause cooking. Flip the Brussels sprout halves and press the "Start/Pause" button to resume cooking.

Step 5: After the cooking time has elapsed, remove the Brussels sprout halves from the air fryer and transfer onto a plate. Set aside to cool.

Step 6: In a serving bowl, mix together the Brussels sprout halves, apples, onion, and lettuce.

Step 7: For the dressing, add all the ingredients in a bowl and beat until well combined. Add the dressing and gently stir to combine. Serve immediately.

Veggie Casserole

Prep. Time
15 minutes

Cooking Time
12 minutes

Yield
6 Servings

A wonderful and easy way to prepare a veggie casserole in your air fryer… The combo of fresh lemon juice, spices, and dried herbs adds just the right amount of flavouring to the veggies. Air fryer cooking also gives a nice texture to the veggies.

Energy value 184 Kcal | Protein 3.6g
Carbohydrates 15.9g | Fats 12.2g

Ingredients:

- Non-stick cooking spray
- 680g fresh green beans, trimmed
- 220g fresh button mushrooms, sliced
- 45ml olive oil
- 60ml fresh lemon juice
- 5g ground sage
- 5g onion powder
- 5g garlic powder
- 65g French fried onions

Instructions:

Step 1: Grease the air fryer basket with cooking spray, then slide it inside.

Step 2: Adjust the temperature of the air fryer to 205 °C to preheat for 5 minutes and press the "Start/Pause" button to start preheating.

Step 3: In a bowl, add the green beans, mushrooms, oil, lemon juice, sage, and spices, and toss to coat well.

Step 4: After preheating, place the mushroom mixture into the preheated air fryer basket.

Step 5: Slide the basket inside and set the timer for 10–12 minutes.

Step 6: Press the "Start/Pause" button to start cooking.

Step 7: After 6 minutes of cooking, press the "Start/Pause" button to pause cooking.

Step 8: Shake the basket and press the "Start/Pause" button to resume cooking.

Step 9: After the cooking time has elapsed, remove the mushroom mixture from the air fryer and transfer into a serving dish.

Step 10: Top with fried onions and serve.

Ratatouille

Prep. Time
15 minutes

Cooking Time
15 minutes

Yield
4 Servings

A Mediterranean-inspired veggie medley for your dining table… This recipe provides an impressive and crowd-pleasing vegetable meal for all… This flavour-packed dish will be a great hit for veggie lovers.

Energy value 120 Kcal | Protein 3.6g
Carbohydrates 20.3g | Fats 4.2g

Ingredients:

- Non-stick cooking spray
- 1 green bell pepper, seeded and chopped
- 1 yellow bell pepper, seeded and chopped
- 1 brinjal, chopped
- 1 courgette, chopped
- 3 tomatoes, chopped
- 2 small onions, chopped
- 2 garlic cloves, minced
- 20g Provençal herbs
- 15ml olive oil
- 15ml balsamic vinegar
- Salt and ground black pepper, as required

Instructions:

Step 1: Grease a baking dish with cooking spray.

Step 2: In a large bowl, add the vegetables, garlic, Provençal herbs, oil, vinegar, salt, and black pepper, and toss to coat well.

Step 3: Place the vegetable mixture into the greased baking dish.

Step 4: Slide the air fryer basket inside and adjust the temperature to 180 ºC to preheat for 5 minutes.

Step 5: Press the "Start/Pause" button to start preheating.

Step 6: After preheating, place the baking dish into the preheated air fryer basket.

Step 7: Slide the basket inside and set the timer for 15 minutes.

Step 8: Press the "Start/Pause" button to start cooking.

Step 9: After the cooking time has elapsed, remove the baking dish from the air fryer and serve hot.

Parmesan Veggies

Prep. Time
15 minutes

Cooking Time
18 minutes

Yield
4 Servings

A delicious addition to your healthy meals menu… These garden-fresh veggies are flavoured with a combo of balsamic vinegar, oil, garlic, and seasoning, then topped with gooey Parmesan cheese. This recipe makes a delicious dish that is filling too.

Energy value 94 Kcal | Protein 4.9g
Carbohydrates 7.9g | Fats 5.6g

Ingredients:

- 100g cauliflower florets
- 90g broccoli florets
- 115g courgette, sliced
- 60g yellow squash, sliced
- 50g fresh mushrooms, sliced
- 1 small onion, sliced
- 60ml balsamic vinegar
- 15ml olive oil
- 5g garlic, minced
- 5g red pepper flakes, crushed
- Salt and ground black pepper, as required
- Non-stick cooking spray
- 30g Parmesan cheese, grated

Instructions:

Step 1: In a large bowl, add all the ingredients except for the cheese and toss to coat well.

Step 2: Grease the air fryer basket with cooking spray, then slide it inside.

Step 3: Adjust the temperature of the air fryer to 90 °C to preheat for 5 minutes and press the "Start/Pause" button to start preheating.

Step 4: After preheating, place the vegetables into the preheated air fryer basket.

Step 5: Slide the basket inside and set the timer for 18 minutes. Press the "Start/Pause" button to start cooking.

Step 6: After the cooking time has elapsed, remove the potatoes from the air fryer.

Step 7: After 8 minutes of cooking, press the "Start/Pause" button to pause cooking.

Step 8: Flip the vegetables and press the "Start/Pause" button to resume cooking.

Step 9: After 16 minutes of cooking, press the "Start/Pause" button to pause cooking.

Step 10: Sprinkle the vegetables with cheese evenly and press the "Start/Pause" button to resume cooking.

Step 11: After the cooking time has elapsed, remove the vegetables from the air fryer and serve hot.

Veggie Pizza

Prep. Time
15 minutes

Cooking Time
15 minutes

Yield
2 Servings

A great and unique twist on traditional pizza with a crust… This pitta bread pizza is the best way to encourage your kids to eat delicious vegetables… This easy-to-prepare veggie pizza is high in healthy nutrients and deliciousness.

Energy value 263 Kcal I Protein 12.3g
Carbohydrates 44g I Fats 5.8g

Ingredients:

- 40g marinara sauce
- 1 wholewheat pitta bread
- 15g fresh baby spinach leaves
- ½ of small plum tomato, cut into 4 slices
- ½ of garlic clove, thinly sliced
- 15g mozzarella cheese, grated
- 10g Parmigiano Reggiano cheese, grated
- Non-stick cooking spray

Instructions:

Step 1: Place the pitta bread onto a plate.

Step 2: Spread marinara sauce over pitta bread evenly.

Step 3: Top with the spinach leaves, followed by tomato slices, garlic, and cheeses.

Step 4: Grease the air fryer basket with cooking spray, then slide it inside.

Step 5: Adjust the temperature of the air fryer to 175 °C to preheat for 5 minutes and press the "Start/Pause" button to start preheating.

Step 6: After preheating, place the pitta bread into the preheated air fryer basket.

Step 7: Slide the basket inside and set the timer for 5 minutes.

Step 8: Press the "Start/Pause" button to start cooking.

Step 9: After the cooking time has elapsed, remove the pizza from the air fryer and serve.

Stuffed Brinjal

Prep. Time
15 minutes

Cooking Time
25 minutes

Yield
2 Servings

An awesome recipe of brinjal… This vegetarian filling of tomato salsa, parsley, lemon juice, and seasoning greatly enhances the flavour of brinjal. These air-fried brinjals taste not only delicious but melt in your mouth too.

Energy value 192 Kcal I Protein 6.7g
Carbohydrates 33.6g I Fats 6.2g

Ingredients:

- Non-stick cooking spray
- 1 large brinjal
- 10ml olive oil, divided
- 10ml fresh lemon juice, divided
- 8 cherry tomatoes, quartered
- 30g tomato salsa
- 5g fresh parsley
- Salt and ground black pepper, as required

Instructions:

Step 1: Grease the air fryer basket with cooking spray, then slide it inside. Adjust the temperature to 200 °C to preheat for 5 minutes. Press the "Start/Pause" button to start preheating.

Step 2: After preheating, place the brinjal into the preheated air fryer basket. Place the brinjal into the preheated air fryer basket.

Step 3: Slide the basket inside and set the timer for 15 minutes. Press the "Start/Pause" button to start cooking.

Step 4: After the cooking time has elapsed, remove the brinjal from the air fryer and place onto a chopping board for about 5 minutes.

Step 5: Cut the brinjal in half lengthwise. Drizzle the brinjal halves evenly with 5ml of oil.

Step 6: Again, grease the air fryer basket with cooking spray, then slide it inside. Adjust the temperature to 180 °C to preheat for 5 minutes. Press the "Start/Pause" button to start preheating.

Step 7: Place the brinjal halves into the preheated air fryer basket, cut-side up. Slide the basket inside and set the timer for 10 minutes. Press the "Start/Pause" button to start cooking.

Step 8: After the cooking time has elapsed, remove the brinjal halves from the air fryer and set aside for about 5 minutes.

Step 9: Carefully scoop out the flesh, leaving about ¼-inch gap from the edges. Drizzle the brinjal halves with 5ml of lemon juice.

Step 10: Transfer the brinjal flesh into a bowl. Add the tomatoes, salsa, parsley, salt, black pepper, remaining oil, and lemon juice, and mix well.

Stuffed Tomatoes

Prep. Time
15 minutes

Cooking Time
15 minutes

Yield
2 Servings

Looking for a fancy and fun recipe to impress guests in your home? This air fryer recipe is the best way to transform tomatoes into an extraordinary feast. These stuffed tomatoes are packed with the taste of broccoli and thyme alongside cheesy goodness.

Energy value 208 Kcal | Protein 9.3g
Carbohydrates 9.7g | Fats 15.7g

Ingredients:

• 2 large tomatoes
• 45g broccoli, finely chopped
• 55g cheddar cheese, grated
• 15g unsalted butter, melted
• 2.5g dried thyme, crushed

Instructions:

Step 1: Slice the top of each tomato and scoop out the pulp and seeds.

Step 2: In a bowl, mix together the chopped broccoli and cheese.

Step 3: Stuff each tomato evenly with the broccoli mixture.

Step 4: Grease the air fryer basket with cooking spray, then slide it inside.

Step 5: Adjust the temperature of the air fryer to 180 °C to preheat for 5 minutes and press the "Start/Pause" button to start preheating.

Step 6: After preheating, place the tomatoes into the preheated air fryer basket and drizzle evenly with butter.

Step 7: Slide the basket inside and set the timer for 12–15 minutes.

Step 8: Press the "Start/Pause" button to start cooking.

Step 9: After the cooking time has elapsed, remove the tomatoes from the air fryer and serve.

Stuffed Pumpkin

Prep. Time
20 minutes

Cooking Time
30 minutes

Yield
4 Servings

One of the best and tastiest vegetarian recipes for cold winter days... This pumpkin is stuffed with a hearty filling of veggies and herbs And is a great addition to your winter menu.

Energy value 157 Kcal | Protein 4.6g
Carbohydrates 35.9g | Fats 1.1g

Ingredients:

• 1 sweet potato, peeled and chopped
• 1 parsnip, peeled and chopped
• 1 carrot, peeled and chopped
• 70g fresh green peas, shelled
• 1 onion, chopped
• 2 garlic cloves, minced
• 1 egg, beaten
• 10g mixed dried herbs
• Salt and ground black pepper, as required
• ½ of butternut pumpkin, seeded

Instructions:

Step 1: Slice the top of each tomato and scoop out the pulp and seeds.

Step 1: In a large bowl, add vegetables, garlic, egg, herbs, salt, and black pepper, and mix well.

Step 2: Stuff the pumpkin half with the vegetable mixture.

Step 3: Grease the air fryer basket with cooking spray, then slide it inside.

Step 4: Adjust the temperature of the air fryer to 180 °C to preheat for 5 minutes and press the "Start/Pause" button to start preheating.

Step 5: After preheating, place the pumpkin half into the preheated air fryer basket and drizzle evenly with butter.

Step 6: Slide the basket inside and set the timer for 30 minutes.

Step 7: Press the "Start/Pause" button to start cooking.

Step 8: After the cooking time has elapsed, remove the pumpkin half from the air fryer and serve warm.

Vegan Recipes

Hello! Please scan the QR code below to access your promised bonus of all our recipes with full colored photos & beautiful designs! It is the best we could do to keep the book as cheap as possible while providing the best value!

Also, once downloaded you can take the PDF with you digitally wherever you go- meaning you can cook these recipes wherever an Air Fryer is present!

STEP BY STEP Guide To Access-

1) Open Your Phones (Or Any Device You Want The Book On) Back Camera. The Back Camera Is The One You use as if you are taking a picture of someone.

2) Simply point your Camera at the QR code and 'tap' the QR code with your finger to focus the camera.

3) A link / pop up will appear. Simply tap that (and make sure you have internet connection) and the FREE PDF containing all of the colored images should appear.

4) If You Click On The File And It Says 'The File Is Too Big To Preview' Simply click 'Download' and it will download the full book onto your phone!

5) Now you have access to these FOREVER. Simply 'Bookmark' The tab it opened on, or download the document and take wherever you want.

6) Repeat this on any device you want it on!

Any Issues / Feedback / Troubleshooting please email: anthonypublishing123@gmail.com and our customer service team will help you! We want to make sure you have the BEST experience with our books!

Dinner Rolls

Prep. Time
20 minutes

Cooking Time
25 minutes

Yield
6 Servings

Have you ever tasted a batch of soft and fluffy homemade dinner rolls without the use of an oven? Then try this air fryer recipe without any hesitation. These vegan-friendly dinner rolls are perfect to serve alongside dinner or lunch.

Energy value 209 Kcal I Protein 3.8g
Carbohydrates 25.3g I Fats 10.6g

Ingredients:

- 120ml unsweetened almond milk
- 50g coconut oil, divided
- 10ml olive oil
- 195g plain flour
- 5g yeast
- Salt and ground black pepper, as required
- Non-stick cooking spray

Instructions:

Step 1: In a saucepan, add the almond milk, 5g of coconut oil, and olive oil, and cook until lukewarm.

Step 2: Remove from the heat and stir well.

Step 3: In a large bowl, add the flour, remaining coconut oil, yeast, salt, black pepper, and milk mixture, and mix until a dough forms.

Step 4: With your hands, knead for about 4–5 minutes.

Step 5: With a damp cloth, cover the dough and set aside in a warm place for about 5 minutes.

Step 6: Again, with your hands, knead the dough for about 4–5 minutes.

Step 7: With a damp cloth, cover the dough and set aside in a warm place for about 30 minutes.

Step 8: Place the dough onto a lightly floured surface.

Step 9: Divide the dough into 6 equal-sized pieces, then shape each into a ball.

Step 10: Grease the air fryer basket with cooking spray, then slide it inside.

Step 11: Adjust the temperature of the air fryer to 185 °C to preheat for 5 minutes.

Step 12: Press the "Start/Pause" button to start preheating.

Step 13: After preheating, place the rolls into the preheated air fryer basket in a single layer.

Step 14: Slide the basket inside and set the timer for 15 minutes. Press the "Start/Pause" button to start cooking.

Step 15: After the cooking time has elapsed, remove the rolls from the air fryer and serve warm.

Veggie Bread Rolls

Prep. Time
20 minutes

Cooking Time
33 minutes

Yield
8 Servings

The best way to prepare delicious bread rolls to perfection… These bread rolls are filled with a delicious savoury filling of perfectly spiced mashed potatoes, onion, and green chillies. Using an air fryer will allow you to prepare these bread rolls without deep frying.

Energy value 256 Kcal I Protein 6.3g
Carbohydrates 49.8g I Fats 4.4g

Ingredients:

- 5 large potatoes, peeled
- 30ml vegetable oil, divided
- 2 small onions, finely chopped
- 2 green chillies, seeded and chopped
- 2 curry leaves
- 2.5g ground turmeric
- Salt, as required
- 8 vegan bread slices, trimmed
- Non-stick cooking spray

Instructions:

Step 1: In the pan of boiling water, add the potatoes and cook for about 15–20 minutes. Drain the potatoes well, and with a potato masher, mash the potatoes.

Step 2: In a skillet, heat 5ml of oil over medium heat and sauté the onion for about 4–5 minutes. Add the green chillies, curry leaves, and turmeric. Sauté for about 1 minute.

Step 3: Add in the mashed potatoes and salt, and mix them well. Once done, remove from the heat and set aside to cool completely.

Step 4: Make 8 equal-sized oval-shaped patties from the mixture.

Step 5: Wet the bread slices completely with water. Press each bread slice between your hands to remove the excess water.

Step 6: Place 1 bread slice in your palm and place 1 patty in the centre. Roll the bread slice in a spindle shape and seal the edges to secure the filling. Coat the roll with some oil.

Step 7: Repeat with the remaining slices, filling, and oil.

Step 8: Grease the air fryer basket with cooking spray, then slide it inside. Adjust the temperature to 200 °C to preheat for 5 minutes and press the "Start/Pause" button to start preheating.

Step 9: After preheating, place the rolls into the preheated air fryer basket in a single layer.

Step 10: Slide the basket inside and set the timer for 12–13 minutes. Press the "Start/Pause" button to start cooking.

Step 11: After the cooking time has elapsed, remove the rolls from the air fryer and serve.

Tofu with Orange Sauce

Prep. Time
15 minutes

Cooking Time
10 minutes

Yield
4 Servings

A homemade meal of bright, citric tofu that's restaurant quality... This crispy tofu is smothered in a sweet and tangy sauce. Your whole family will enjoy this cosy meal.

Energy value 162 Kcal | Protein 12.2g
Carbohydrates 15.8g | Fats 6.8g

Ingredients:

For Tofu:

- 455g extra-firm tofu, pressed and cubed
- 15g cornflour
- 15ml tamari
- Non-stick cooking spray

For Sauce:

- 120ml water
- 90ml fresh orange juice
- 20g maple syrup
- 5g orange zest, grated
- 5g garlic, minced
- 5g fresh ginger, minced
- 10g cornflour
- 1.25g red pepper flakes, crushed

Instructions:

Step 1: In a bowl, add the tofu, cornflour, and tamari, and toss to coat well.

Step 2: Set the tofu aside to marinate for at least 15 minutes.

Step 3: Grease the air fryer basket with cooking spray, then slide it inside.

Step 4: Adjust the temperature of the air fryer to 200 °C to preheat for 5 minutes. Press the "Start/Pause" button to start preheating.

Step 5: After preheating, place the tofu cubes into the preheated air fryer basket in a single layer.

Step 6: Slide the basket inside and set the timer for 10 minutes. Press the "Start/Pause" button to start cooking.

Step 7: After 5 minutes of cooking, press the "Start/Pause" button to pause cooking. Flip the tofu cubes and press the "Start/Pause" button to resume cooking.

Step 8: For the sauce, add all the ingredients in a small pan over medium-high heat and bring to a boil, stirring continuously.

Step 9: After the cooking time has elapsed, remove the tofu cubes from the air fryer and transfer into a serving bowl. Add the sauce and gently stir to combine.

Step 10: Serve immediately

Tofu with Cauliflower

Prep. Time
15 minutes

Cooking Time
15 minutes

Yield
2 Servings

The perfect vegetarian recipe for the whole family... This dish helps you get a great dose of tofu and cauliflower with added flavour and nutrients. The homemade seasoning blend adds a wholesome flavouring to the tofu and cauliflower.

Energy value 170 Kcal | Protein 11.6g
Carbohydrates 8.3g | Fats 11.9g

Ingredients:

- Non-stick cooking spray
- 595g firm tofu, pressed and cubed
- 10g nutritional yeast
- 5g ground turmeric
- Salt and ground black pepper, as required
- ½ of small head cauliflower, cut into florets
- 15ml canola oil
- 1.25g dried parsley
- 1.25g paprika

Instructions:

Step 1: In a bowl, add in tofu, cauliflower, and the remaining ingredients, and mix well.

Step 2: Grease the air fryer basket with cooking spray, then slide it inside.

Step 3: Adjust the temperature to 200 °C to preheat for 5 minutes.

Step 4: Press the "Start/Pause" button to start preheating.

Step 5: After preheating, place the tofu mixture into the preheated air fryer basket in a single layer.

Step 6: Slide the basket inside and set the timer for 12–15 minutes.

Step 7: Press the "Start/Pause" button to start cooking.

Step 8: While cooking, shake the basket once halfway through.

Step 9: After the cooking time has elapsed, remove the tofu from the air fryer and serve hot.

Rice- and Bean- Stuffed Bell Peppers

Prep. Time
15 minutes

Cooking Time
15 minutes

Yield
5 Servings

A family favourite recipe of fancy stuffed bell peppers... These bell peppers are stuffed with a delicious combo of red kidney beans, rice, sweetcorn, tomatoes, and Italian seasoning. These grain-stuffed bell peppers is the perfect lunch for vegans.

Energy value 204 Kcal | Protein 8.5g
Carbohydrates 40.3g | Fats 2.6g

Ingredients:

- ½ of small bell pepper, seeded and chopped
- 1 can diced tomatoes with juice (425g)
- 225g canned red kidney beans, rinsed and drained
- 150g frozen sweetcorn, thawed
- 75g cooked rice
- 5g Italian seasoning
- 5 large bell peppers, tops removed and seeded
- Non-stick cooking spray

Instructions:

Step 1: In a bowl, mix together the chopped bell pepper, tomatoes with juice, beans, rice, and Italian seasoning.

Step 2: Stuff each bell pepper with the rice mixture.

Step 3: Grease the air fryer basket with cooking spray, then slide it inside.

Step 4: Adjust the temperature of the air fryer to 185 °C to preheat for 5 minutes.

Step 5: Press the "Start/Pause" button to start preheating.

Step 6: After preheating, place the bell peppers into the preheated air fryer basket.

Step 7: Slide the basket inside and set the timer for 15 minutes.

Step 8: Press the "Start/Pause" button to start cooking.

Step 9: After the cooking time has elapsed, remove the bell peppers from the air fryer and serve.

Oatmeal-Stuffed Bell Peppers

Prep. Time
15 minutes

Cooking Time
16 minutes

Yield
2 Servings

A delicious recipe of stuffed bell peppers that looks beautiful too... The combo of oatmeal, black beans, coconut yoghurt, and seasoning provides a flavoursome stuffing for the bell peppers. Your family will enjoy these stuffed bell peppers.

Energy value 162 Kcal | Protein 7.7g
Carbohydrates 26.1g | Fats 4.4g

Ingredients:

- Non-stick cooking spray
- 2 large bell peppers, halved lengthwise and seeded
- 160g cooked oatmeal
- 55g canned black beans, rinsed and drained
- 70g coconut yoghurt
- 1.25g smoked paprika
- 1.25g ground cumin
- Salt and ground black pepper, as required

Instructions:

Step 1: Grease the air fryer basket with cooking spray, then slide it inside. Adjust the temperature to 180 °C to preheat for 5 minutes. Press the "Start/Pause" button to start preheating.

Step 2: After preheating, place the bell peppers into the preheated air fryer basket, cut-side down.

Step 3: Slide the basket inside and set the timer for 8 minutes.

Step 4: After the cooking time has elapsed, remove the bell peppers from the air fryer and set aside to cool.

Step 5: Meanwhile, in a bowl, mix well the oatmeal, beans, coconut yoghurt, and spices.

Step 6: Stuff each bell pepper half with the oatmeal mixture.

Step 7: Again, grease the air fryer basket with cooking spray, then slide it inside.

Step 8: Adjust the temperature to 180 °C to preheat for 5 minutes. Press the "Start/Pause" button to start preheating.

Step 9: After preheating, place the stuffed bell peppers into the preheated air fryer basket.

Step 10: Slide the basket inside and set the timer for 8 minutes. Press the "Start/Pause" button to start cooking.

Step 11: After the cooking time has elapsed, remove the bell peppers from the air fryer and place onto a serving platter.

Step 12: Set aside to cool slightly before serving.

Rice-Stuffed Tomatoes

Prep. Time
15 minutes

Cooking Time
20 minutes

Yield
4 Servings

One of the most attractive and tasty lunch treats… These tomatoes are stuffed with cooked rice, green peas, carrot, and seasoning, then cooked in the air fryer to perfection. This stuffed tomato recipe is also a great choice for special family parties.

Energy value 172 Kcal | Protein 5.6g
Carbohydrates 34.3g | Fats 1.8g

Ingredients:

- 4 large tomatoes
- 5ml olive oil
- 1 carrot, peeled and finely chopped
- 1 onion, chopped
- 1 garlic clove, minced
- 145g frozen green peas, thawed
- 280g cold cooked rice
- 15ml soy sauce
- Non-stick cooking spray

Instructions:

Step 1: Cut the top of each tomato and scoop out the pulp and seeds.

Step 2: In a skillet, heat the oil over low heat and sauté the carrot, onion, garlic, and peas for about 2 minutes.

Step 3: Stir in the soy sauce and rice, and remove from the heat.

Step 4: Stuff each tomato with the rice mixture.

Step 5: Grease the air fryer basket with cooking spray, then slide it inside.

Step 6: Adjust the temperature to 180 °C to preheat for 5 minutes.

Step 7: Press the "Start/Pause" button to start preheating.

Step 8: After preheating, place the tomatoes into the preheated air fryer basket.

Step 9: Slide the basket inside and set the timer for 20 minutes.

Step 10: Press the "Start/Pause" button to start cooking.

Step 11: After the cooking time has elapsed, remove the tomatoes from the air fryer and transfer onto a serving platter to cool slightly.

Step 12: Serve warm.

Veggie Bean Burgers

Prep. Time
15 minutes

Cooking Time
21 minutes

Yield
4 Servings

One of the most attractive and tasty lunch treats… These tomatoes are stuffed A recipe of mouthwatering vegetarian burgers… This combo of black beans, potatoes, spinach, and lime seasoning makes these burgers so much tastier. These veggie bean burgers are great when served with a plate of fresh crunchy salad and ketchup.

Energy value 121 Kcal | Protein 26.2g
Carbohydrates 24.3g | Fats 0.4g

Ingredients:

- 170g cooked black beans
- 330g boiled potatoes, peeled and mashed
- 30g fresh spinach, chopped
- 100g fresh mushrooms, chopped
- 10g chilli and lime seasoning
- Non-stick cooking spray

Instructions:

Step 1: In a large bowl, add the beans, potatoes, spinach, mushrooms, and seasoning; and with your hands, mix until well combined.

Step 2: Make 4 equal-sized patties from the mixture.

Step 3: Grease the air fryer basket with cooking spray, then slide it inside.

Step 4: Adjust the temperature of the air fryer to 190 °C to preheat for 5 minutes.

Step 5: Press the "Start/Pause" button to start preheating.

Step 6: After preheating, place the patties into the preheated air fryer basket in a single layer and spray with the cooking spray.

Step 7: Slide the basket inside and set the timer for 18 minutes.

Step 8: Press the "Start/Pause" button to start cooking.

Step 9: After 12 minutes of cooking, press the "Start/Pause" button to pause cooking.

Step 10: Flip the patties and spray with the cooking spray.

Step 11: Again, press the "Start/Pause" button to resume cooking.

Step 12: After 18 minutes of cooking, adjust the temperature to 90 °C for 3 minutes.

Step 13: After the cooking time has elapsed, remove the burgers from the air fryer and serve hot.

Chickpea Falafels

Prep. Time
15 minutes

Cooking Time
15 minutes

Yield
3 Servings

The best recipe to prepare restaurant-quality falafels at home… The chickpeas are perfectly flavoured with seasoning and lemon, then shaped into perfect falafels. Air fryer cooking gives a wonderful texture to these falafels.

Energy value 221 Kcal | Protein 8.9g
Carbohydrates 39.2g | Fats 3.9g

Ingredients:

- 1 can chickpeas, rinsed and drained (425g)
- 10g fresh coriander
- 10g fresh parsley
- 1 garlic clove, peeled
- ½ of large shallot, chopped
- 15g plain flour
- 10g sesame seeds
- 5ml fresh lemon juice
- 5g ground cumin
- 2.5g paprika
- Salt, as required
- Non-stick cooking spray

Instructions:

Step 1: In a food processor, add all the ingredients and pulse until the mixture comes together in a rough paste.

Step 2: Make small-sized balls from the mixture, and then with your fingers, flatten each slightly.

Step 3: Grease the air fryer basket with cooking spray, then slide it inside.

Step 4: Adjust the temperature of the air fryer to 175 °C to preheat for 5 minutes.

Step 5: Press the "Start/Pause" button to start preheating.

Step 6: After preheating, place the falafels into the preheated air fryer basket in a single layer.

Step 7: Slide the basket inside and set the timer for 14 minutes.

Step 8: Press the "Start/Pause" button to start cooking.

Step 9: After 7 minutes of cooking, press the "Start/Pause" button to pause cooking.

Step 10: Flip the falafels and press the "Start/Pause" button to resume cooking.

Step 11: After the cooking time has elapsed, remove the falafels from the air fryer and serve.

Veggie Rice

Prep. Time
15 minutes

Cooking Time
15 minutes

Yield
2 Servings

Have you ever imagined making a delicious plate of rice in an air fryer? After following this recipe, you will be able to prepare a scrumptious rice and veggie platter for the whole family… Your kids will also love this veggie rice dish.

Energy value 332 Kcal | Protein 6.4g
Carbohydrates 47.5g | Fats 12.8g

Ingredients:

- 280g cooked white rice
- 15ml vegetable oil
- 10ml sesame oil, toasted and divided
- 15ml water
- Salt and ground white pepper, as required
- 75g frozen green peas, thawed
- 45g frozen carrots, thawed
- 5ml light soy sauce
- 3g sesame seeds, toasted
- 5ml sriracha sauce

Instructions:

Step 1: Lightly grease the air fryer pan with cooking spray, then slide it inside.

Step 2: Adjust the temperature of the air fryer to 195 °C to preheat for 5 minutes.

Step 3: In a large bowl, add the rice, vegetable oil, 5ml of sesame oil, water, salt, and white pepper, and mix well.

Step 4: Press the "Start/Pause" button to start preheating.

Step 5: After preheating, place the rice mixture into the preheated air fryer pan.

Step 6: Slide the pan inside and set the timer for 18 minutes.

Step 7: Press the "Start/Pause" button to start cooking.

Step 8: After 6 minutes of cooking, press the "Start/Pause" button to pause cooking.

Step 9: Stir the rice mixture and press the "Start/Pause" button to resume cooking. After 15 minutes of cooking, press the "Start/Pause" button to pause cooking.

Step 10: Add the peas and carrots in the pan with the rice mixture and stir to combine. Again, press the "Start/Pause" button to resume cooking.

Step 11: Meanwhile, in a bowl, mix together the soy sauce, sriracha sauce, sesame seeds, and the remaining sesame oil.

Step 12: After the cooking time has elapsed, remove the rice mixture from the air fryer and transfer into a serving bowl.

Step 13: Drizzle with the sauce mixture and serve.

Side Dishes Recipes

Hello! Please scan the QR code below to access your promised bonus of all our recipes with full colored photos & beautiful designs! It is the best we could do to keep the book as cheap as possible while providing the best value!

Also, once downloaded you can take the PDF with you digitally wherever you go- meaning you can cook these recipes wherever an Air Fryer is present!

STEP BY STEP Guide To Access-

1) Open Your Phones (Or Any Device You Want The Book On) Back Camera. The Back Camera Is The One You use as if you are taking a picture of someone.

2) Simply point your Camera at the QR code and 'tap' the QR code with your finger to focus the camera.

3) A link / pop up will appear. Simply tap that (and make sure you have internet connection) and the FREE PDF containing all of the colored images should appear.

4) If You Click On The File And It Says 'The File Is Too Big To Preview' Simply click 'Download' and it will download the full book onto your phone!

5) Now you have access to these FOREVER. Simply 'Bookmark' The tab it opened on, or download the document and take wherever you want.

6) Repeat this on any device you want it on!

Any Issues / Feedback / Troubleshooting please email: anthonypublishing123@gmail.com and our customer service team will help you! We want to make sure you have the BEST experience with our books!

Hasselback Potatoes

Prep. Time
15 minutes

Cooking Time
30 minutes

Yield
4 Servings

Do you want to enjoy delicious, beautiful potatoes? This is an impressive side dish that's perfect for weekend meals! These beautifully sliced potatoes are enhanced with the taste of butter, chives, and cheese.

Energy value 220 Kcal | Protein 4.8g
Carbohydrates 33.6g | Fats 8.1g

Ingredients:

- 4 potatoes
- Non-stick cooking spray
- 30g butter, melted
- 15g Parmesan cheese, grated
- 3g fresh chives, chopped

Instructions:

Step 1: With a sharp knife, cut slits along each potato the short way about ¼-inch apart, making sure the slices stay connected at the bottom.

Step 2: Grease the air fryer basket with cooking spray, then slide it inside.

Step 3: Adjust the temperature of the air fryer to 180 °C to preheat for 5 minutes.

Step 4: Press the "Start/Pause" button to start preheating.

Step 5: After preheating, place the potatoes into the preheated air fryer basket in a single layer.

Step 6: Slide the basket into the air fryer and set the timer for 30 minutes.

Step 7: Press the "Start/Pause" button to start cooking.

Step 8: After 15 minutes of cooking, press the "Start/Pause" button to pause cooking.

Step 9: Coat the potatoes with melted butter and press the "Start/Pause" button to resume cooking.

Step 10: After the cooking time has elapsed, remove the potatoes from the air fryer and place onto a platter.

Step 11: Garnish with the cheese and chives and serve immediately.

Cheesy Spinach

Prep. Time
15 minutes

Cooking Time
15 minutes

Yield
4 Servings

A healthy side dish of spinach… This plate is packed with a medley of cream cheese, Parmesan cheese, and seasoning. You can boost the flavour of this rich, cheesy spinach with a sprinkling of French fried onions.

Energy value 194 Kcal | Protein 7.4g
Carbohydrates 7.3g | Fats 15.5g

Ingredients:

- 1 packet frozen spinach, thawed (285g)
- 60g onion, chopped
- 5g garlic, minced
- 115g cream cheese, chopped
- 2.5g ground nutmeg
- Salt and ground black pepper, as required
- Non-stick cooking spray
- 30g Parmesan cheese, grated

Instructions:

Step 1: In a bowl, add the spinach, onion, garlic, cream cheese, nutmeg, salt, and black pepper, and mix well.

Step 2: Grease the air fryer pan with cooking spray, then slide it inside.

Step 3: Adjust the temperature of the air fryer to 175 °C to preheat for 5 minutes.

Step 4: After preheating, place the spinach mixture into the preheated air fryer pan.

Step 5: Slide the pan inside and set the timer for 10 minutes.

Step 6: Press the "Start/Pause" button to start cooking.

Step 7: After 10 minutes of cooking, press the "Start/Pause" button to pause cooking.

Step 8: Sprinkle the spinach mixture evenly with Parmesan cheese.

Step 9: Again, press the "Start/Pause" button to resume cooking.

Step 10: After the cooking time has elapsed, remove the spinach mixture from the air fryer and serve hot.

Goat Cheese Kale

Prep. Time
15 minutes

Cooking Time
15 minutes

Yield
4 Servings

A plate of fresh kale, being a superfood, serves as the best side dish… This air fryer recipe sees you preparing one of the most perfect side dishes to accompany main dishes comprising meat or seafood. Lemon juice and goat cheese enhance the flavour of the kale nicely.

Energy value 272 Kcal | Protein 11.8g
Carbohydrates 12.5g | Fats 20.5g

Ingredients:

- Non-stick cooking spray
- 455g fresh kale, tough ribs removed and chopped
- 45ml olive oil
- Salt and ground black pepper, as required
- 110g goat cheese, crumbled
- 5ml fresh lemon juice

Instructions:

Step 1: Grease the air fryer basket with cooking spray, then slide it inside.

Step 2: Adjust the temperature to 170 °C to preheat for 5 minutes and press the "Start/Pause" button to start preheating.

Step 3: In a bowl, add the kale, oil, salt, and black pepper, and mix well.

Step 4: After preheating, place the kale into the preheated air fryer basket.

Step 5: Slide the basket inside and set the timer for 15 minutes.

Step 6: Press the "Start/Pause" button to start cooking.

Step 7: After the cooking time has elapsed, remove the kale from the air fryer and transfer the kale mixture into a bowl.

Step 8: Immediately stir in the cheese and lemon juice.

Step 9: Serve hot.

Caramelised Baby Carrots

Prep. Time
15 minutes

Cooking Time
15 minutes

Yield
2 Servings

A simple yet yummy side dish of tender and sweet baby carrots… The baby carrots are beautifully glazed, then roasted in an air fryer until perfectly tender. The butter and brown sugar caramelises the baby carrots.

Energy value 416 Kcal | Protein 1.3g
Carbohydrates 36.2g | Fats 20g

Ingredients:

- 115g butter, melted
- 100g brown sugar
- 1 small bag baby carrots
- Non-stick cooking spray

Instructions:

Step 1: Grease the air fryer basket with cooking spray, then slide it inside.

Step 2: Adjust the temperature to 205 °C to preheat for 5 minutes and press the "Start/Pause" button to start preheating.

Step 3: In a bowl, mix together the butter and brown sugar.

Step 4: Add the carrots and coat well.

Step 5: After preheating, place the carrots into the preheated air fryer basket in a single layer.

Step 6: Slide the basket inside and set the timer for 15 minutes.

Step 7: Press the "Start/Pause" button to start cooking.

Step 8: After the cooking time has elapsed, remove the carrots from the air fryer and serve hot.

Prep. Time
15 minutes

Cooking Time
10 minutes

Yield
2 Servings

Parmesan Brussels Sprout

One of the best ways to prepare Brussels sprouts as a side for lavish dinner meals… These Parmesan Brussels sprouts accompany meat entrees nicely. These delicious Parmesan Brussels sprouts will be an amazing addition to your holiday table.

Energy value 169 Kcal | Protein 9.7g
Carbohydrates 20.2g | Fats 7.6g

Ingredients:

- Non-stick cooking spray
- 455g Brussels sprouts, trimmed and halved
- Salt and ground black pepper, as required
- 30g Parmesan cheese, grated
- 15ml balsamic vinegar
- 15ml extra-virgin olive oil
- 25g wholewheat breadcrumbs

Instructions:

Step 1: Grease the air fryer basket with cooking spray, then slide it inside.

Step 2: Adjust the temperature to 205 °C to preheat for 5 minutes and press the "Start/Pause" button to start preheating.

Step 3: In a bowl, add the Brussel sprouts, vinegar, oil, salt, and black pepper, and mix well.

Step 4: After preheating, place the Brussels sprouts into the preheated air fryer basket in a single layer.

Step 5: Slide the basket inside and set the timer for 10 minutes.

Step 6: Press the "Start/Pause" button to start cooking.

Step 7: After 5 minutes of cooking, press the "Start/Pause" button to pause cooking.

Step 8: Flip the Brussel sprouts and sprinkle with breadcrumbs, followed by the cheese.

Step 9: Again, press the "Start/Pause" button to resume cooking.

Step 10: After the cooking time has elapsed, remove the Brussels sprouts from the air fryer and serve hot.

Prep. Time
15 minutes

Cooking Time
20 minutes

Yield
4 Servings

Spiced Butternut Squash

An impressive side dish recipe of the air fryer roasted butternut squash… The simple spice combo enhances the taste of nutritious butternut squash. This impressive side dish of spicy butternut squash is a great choice for dinners and impromptu gatherings.

Energy value 144 Kcal | Protein 2.9g
Carbohydrates 28.1g | Fats 2.9g

Ingredients:

- Non-stick cooking spray
- 1 medium butternut squash, peeled, seeded, and cut into chunks
- 10g cumin seeds
- 1.25g garlic powder
- 1.25g chilli flakes, crushed
- Salt and ground black pepper, as required
- 15ml olive oil
- 5g fresh coriander, chopped

Instructions:

Step 1: Grease the air fryer basket with cooking spray, then slide it inside.

Step 2: Adjust the temperature to 190 °C to preheat for 5 minutes and press the "Start/Pause" button to start preheating.

Step 3: In a bowl, mix together the squash, spices, and oil.

Step 4: After preheating, place the squash chunks into the preheated air fryer basket.

Step 5: Slide the basket inside and set the timer for 20 minutes.

Step 6: Press the "Start/Pause" button to start cooking.

Step 7: After 10 minutes of cooking, press the "Start/Pause" button to pause cooking.

Step 8: Flip the squash chunks and press the "Start/Pause" button to resume cooking.

Step 9: After the cooking time has elapsed, remove the squash chunks from the air fryer and serve.

Spiced Sweet Potato

Prep. Time
15 minutes

Cooking Time
20 minutes

Yield
4 Servings

A healthy veggie choice for winter special dinner meals of meat... Sweet potatoes are coated in a mixture of oil, dried parsley, and spices, then roasted in a hot air fryer until brown and crispy. This spiced sweet potato plate will be loved by the whole family.

Energy value 198 Kcal | Protein1.9g
Carbohydrates 32g | Fats 7.3g

Ingredients:

- Non-stick cooking spray
- 3 large sweet potatoes, peeled and cut into 1-inch cubes
- 30ml vegetable oil
- Pinch of dried parsley
- 2.5g ground cumin
- 2.5g red chilli powder
- Salt and ground black pepper, as required

Instructions:

Step 1: Grease the air fryer basket with cooking spray, then slide it inside.

Step 2: Adjust the temperature to 205 °C to preheat for 5 minutes and press the "Start/Pause" button to start preheating.

Step 3: In a large bowl, add all the ingredients and toss to coat well.

Step 4: After preheating, place the sweet potato cubes into the preheated air fryer basket.

Step 5: Slide the basket inside and set the timer for 20 minutes.

Step 6: Press the "Start/Pause" button to start cooking.

Step 7: After the cooking time has elapsed, remove the sweet potato cubes from the air fryer and serve hot.

Braised Mushrooms

Prep. Time
15 minutes

Cooking Time
30 minutes

Yield
6 Servings

A side dish of braised mushrooms that is delicious and super-nutritious... This dish is packed with the delicious goodness of mushrooms. The healthy mushrooms are flavoured with a combo of butter, Provençal herbs, garlic powder, and white wine.

Energy value 56 Kcal | Protein 4.8g
Carbohydrates 5.4g | Fats 2.5g

Ingredients:

- 15g butter
- 10g Provençal herbs
- 2.5g garlic powder
- 910g fresh mushrooms, quartered
- 30ml white wine

Instructions:

Step 1: In the air fryer pan, mix together the butter, Provençal herbs, and garlic powder.

Step 2: Slide the air fryer pan inside and adjust the temperature to 160 °C.

Step 3: Press the "Start/Pause" button to start cooking.

Step 4: After 2 minutes of cooking, press the "Start/Pause" button to pause cooking.

Step 5: In the pan, add the mushrooms and stir to combine.

Step 6: Again, press the "Start/Pause" button to resume cooking.

Step 7: After 26 minutes of cooking, press the "Start/Pause" button to pause cooking.

Step 8: In the pan, add the wine and stir to combine.

Step 9: Again, press the "Start/Pause" button to resume cooking.

Step 10: After the cooking time has elapsed, remove the mushroom mixture from the air fryer and serve hot.

Vinegar Broccoli

Prep. Time
10 minutes

Cooking Time
20 minutes

Yield
2 Servings

A super-tasty recipe of broccoli for a healthy side dish… The combo of balsamic vinegar, oil, and seasoning gives a wonderful flavour to the broccoli. This deliciously seasoned broccoli is great when served alongside roasted chicken, beef, or fish dishes.

Energy value 130 Kcal | Protein 4.5g
Carbohydrates 8.3g | Fats 5.3g

Ingredients:

- 285g frozen broccoli
- 45ml balsamic vinegar
- 15ml olive oil
- 1.25g cayenne powder
- Salt and ground black pepper, as required

Instructions:

Step 1: Grease the air fryer basket with cooking spray, then slide it inside.

Step 2: Adjust the temperature to 205 °C to preheat for 5 minutes and press the "Start/Pause" button to start preheating.

Step 3: In a bowl, add the broccoli, vinegar, oil, cayenne, salt, and black pepper, and toss to coat well.

Step 4: After preheating, place the broccoli into the preheated air fryer basket.

Step 5: Slide the basket inside and set the timer for 20 minutes.

Step 6: Press the "Start/Pause" button to start cooking.

Step 7: After 10 minutes of cooking, press the "Start/Pause" button to pause cooking.

Step 8: Shake the basket and press the "Start/Pause" button to resume cooking.

Step 9: After the cooking time has elapsed, remove the broccoli from the air fryer and serve hot.

Lemony Green Beans

Prep. Time
15 minutes

Cooking Time
15 minutes

Yield
2 Servings

One of the best side dishes with fewer calories… This lemony side dish of green beans is a great option for weight watchers. The fresh green beans are flavoured with a combo of butter, fresh lemon juice, and garlic powder, then cooked in the air fryer.

Energy value 587 Kcal | Protein 2.2g
Carbohydrates 8.6g | Fats 2.2g

Ingredients:

- Non-stick cooking spray
- 225g green beans, trimmed and halved
- 5g butter, melted
- 15ml fresh lemon juice
- 1.25g garlic powder
- Salt and ground black pepper, as required

Instructions:

Step 1: Grease the air fryer basket with cooking spray, then slide it inside.

Step 2: Adjust the temperature of the air fryer to 90 °C to preheat for 5 minutes.

Step 3: In a large bowl, add all the ingredients and toss to coat well.

Step 4: Press the "Start/Pause" button to start preheating.

Step 5: After preheating, place the green beans into the preheated air fryer basket in a single layer.

Step 6: Slide the basket into the air fryer and set the timer for 12 minutes.

Step 7: Press the "Start/Pause" button to start cooking.

Step 8: After the cooking time has elapsed, remove the green beans from the air fryer and serve immediately.

Snacks Recipes

Hello! Please scan the QR code below to access your promised bonus of all our recipes with full colored photos & beautiful designs! It is the best we could do to keep the book as cheap as possible while providing the best value!

Also, once downloaded you can take the PDF with you digitally wherever you go- meaning you can cook these recipes wherever an Air Fryer is present!

STEP BY STEP Guide To Access-

1) Open Your Phones (Or Any Device You Want The Book On) Back Camera. The Back Camera Is The One You use as if you are taking a picture of someone.

2) Simply point your Camera at the QR code and 'tap' the QR code with your finger to focus the camera.

3) A link / pop up will appear. Simply tap that (and make sure you have internet connection) and the FREE PDF containing all of the colored images should appear.

4) If You Click On The File And It Says 'The File Is Too Big To Preview' Simply click 'Download' and it will download the full book onto your phone!

5) Now you have access to these FOREVER. Simply 'Bookmark' The tab it opened on, or download the document and take wherever you want.

6) Repeat this on any device you want it on!

Any Issues / Feedback / Troubleshooting please email: anthonypublishing123@gmail.com and our customer service team will help you! We want to make sure you have the BEST experience with our books!

Roasted Cashews

Prep. Time
10 minutes

Cooking Time
5 minutes

Yield
8 Servings

This is one of the easiest and simplest recipes to prepare roasted cashews… This combo of ingredients adds a delicious touch to the cashews. Raw cashews are mixed with melted butter, salt, and black pepper, then roasted in the air fryer to crunchy perfection.

Energy value 201 Kcal I Protein 16.4g
Carbohydrates 11.2g I Fats 10g

Ingredients:

- Non-stick cooking spray
- 260g raw cashews
- 10g butter, melted
- Salt and ground black pepper, as required

Instructions:

Step 1: Grease the air fryer basket with cooking spray, then slide it inside.

Step 2: Adjust the temperature to 180 ℃ to preheat for 5 minutes and press the "Start/Pause" button to start preheating.

Step 3: In a bowl, mix together all the ingredients.

Step 4: After preheating, place the cashews into the preheated air fryer basket.

Step 5: Slide the basket inside and set the timer for 5 minutes.

Step 6: Press the "Start/Pause" button to start cooking.

Step 7: After 2 minutes of cooking, press the "Start/Pause" button to pause cooking.

Step 8: Shake the cashews well and press the "Start/Pause" button to resume cooking.

Step 9: After the cooking time has elapsed, remove the cashews from the air fryer and transfer into a glass bowl.

Step 10: Set aside to cool completely before serving.

Roasted Peanuts

Prep. Time
5 minutes

Cooking Time
15 minutes

Yield
4 Servings

A bowl of crunchy roasted peanuts is one of the best and easiest snacks for any season of the year… Air fryer cooking gives a wonderful texture to the peanuts. Raw peanuts are coated with oil and salt, then finished in the air fryer with a perfectly crunchy texture.

Energy value 214 Kcal I Protein 9.7g
Carbohydrates 6.1g I Fats 18.6g

Ingredients:

- 150g raw peanuts
- 10ml olive oil
- Salt, as required

Instructions:

Step 1: Grease the air fryer basket with cooking spray, then slide it inside.

Step 2: Adjust the temperature to 180 ℃ to preheat for 5 minutes and press the "Start/Pause" button to start preheating.

Step 3: After preheating, place the peanuts into the preheated air fryer basket.

Step 4: Slide the basket inside and set the timer for 15 minutes.

Step 5: Press the "Start/Pause" button to start cooking.

Step 6: After 9 minutes of cooking, press the "Start/Pause" button to pause cooking.

Step 7: Transfer the peanuts into a large bowl with oil, and salt and toss to coat well.

Step 8: Return the peanuts into the air fryer basket and insert into the air fryer.

Step 9: Again, press the "Start/Pause" button to resume cooking.

Step 10: After the cooking time has elapsed, remove the peanuts from the air fryer and transfer into a glass bowl.

Step 11: Set aside to cool completely before serving.

Apple Chips

Prep. Time
10 minutes

Cooking Time
8 minutes

Yield
2 Servings

Have you ever tried making your very own homemade apple chips? This flavourful recipe of spiced apple chips will perfectly satisfy you. The combo of warm spices enhances the flavour of the apple chips in a great way.

Energy value 81 Kcal | Protein 0.4g
Carbohydrates 21.6g | Fats 0.2g

Ingredients:

- Non-stick cooking spray
- 1 apple, peeled, cored, and thinly sliced
- 10g sugar
- 2.5g ground cinnamon
- Pinch of ground cardamom
- Pinch of ground ginger
- Pinch of salt

Instructions:

Step 1: Grease the air fryer basket with cooking spray, then slide it inside.

Step 2: Adjust the temperature to 200 °C to preheat for 5 minutes.

Step 3: Press the "Start/Pause" button to start preheating.

Step 4: In a bowl, add all the ingredients and toss to coat well.

Step 5: After preheating, place the apple slices into the preheated air fryer basket in a single layer.

Step 6: Slide the basket inside and set the timer for 7–8 minutes.

Step 7: Press the "Start/Pause" button to start cooking.

Step 8: After 4 minutes of cooking, press the "Start/Pause" button to pause cooking.

Step 9: Flip the apple slices and press the "Start/Pause" button to resume cooking.

Step 10: After the cooking time has elapsed, remove the apple chips from the air fryer and serve.

French Fries

Prep. Time
15 minutes

Cooking Time
30 minutes

Yield
4 Servings

A mildly spicy air fryer-roasted French fries recipe… You can easily prepare these fries at home in your air fryer. This spicy batch of homemade French fries will please your friends and family, especially your little ones who will ask for these fries again and again.

Energy value 132 Kcal | Protein 1.8g
Carbohydrates 16.2g | Fats 7.3g

Ingredients:

- 795g potatoes, peeled and cut into strips
- 60ml olive oil
- 10g paprika
- 2.5g onion powder
- 2.5g garlic powder
- Non-stick cooking spray

Instructions:

Step 1: In a large bowl of water, add the potato strips and set aside for about 1 hour.

Step 2: Drain the potato strips well and pat them dry with paper towels.

Step 3: In a large bowl, add the potato strips and the remaining ingredients, and toss to coat well.

Step 4: Grease the air fryer basket with cooking spray, then slide it inside.

Step 5: Adjust the temperature to 190 °C to preheat for 5 minutes.

Step 6: Press the "Start/Pause" button to start preheating.

Step 7: After preheating, place the potato strips into the preheated air fryer basket in a single layer.

Step 8: Slide the basket inside and set the timer for 30 minutes.

Step 9: Press the "Start/Pause" button to start cooking.

Step 10: After the cooking time has elapsed, remove the French fries from the air fryer and serve.

Onion Rings

Prep. Time
15 minutes

Cooking Time
10 minutes

Yield
4 Servings

Have you ever enjoyed onion in a different yet tasty way? This is one of the best recipes of crispy onion slices for kids and adults… These crispy onion rings are prepared without the use of extra oil. All your family will demand these crispy onion rings again and again.

Energy value 285 Kcal | Protein 10.5g
Carbohydrates 51.6g | Fats 3.8g

Ingredients:

- 1 large onion, cut into 0.6cm slices
- 160g plain flour
- 4g baking powder
- Salt, as required
- 240ml milk
- 1 egg
- 75g dry breadcrumbs
- Non-stick cooking spray

Instructions:

Step 1: Separate the onion slices into rings.

Step 2: In a shallow dish, mix together the flour, baking powder, and salt.

Step 3: In a second dish, add milk and egg, and mix well.

Step 4: In a third dish, place the breadcrumbs.

Step 5: Coat each onion ring with the flour mixture and dip into the egg mixture. Then coat evenly with the breadcrumbs.

Step 6: Grease the air fryer basket with cooking spray, then slide it inside.

Step 7: Adjust the temperature to 185 °C to preheat for 5 minutes.

Step 8: Press the "Start/Pause" button to start preheating.

Step 9: After preheating, place the onion rings into the preheated air fryer basket in a single layer.

Step 10: Slide the basket inside and set the timer for 7–10 minutes.

Step 11: Press the "Start/Pause" button to start cooking.

Step 12: After the cooking time has elapsed, remove the onion rings from the air fryer and serve hot.

Mozzarella Sticks

Prep. Time
15 minutes

Cooking Time
12 minutes

Yield
4 Servings

One of the most delicious homemade snack recipes… These homemade freshly air-fried mozzarella sticks are surprisingly easy to make and wonderfully gooey. The coating of breadcrumbs and flour gives a crunchiness to the mozzarella sticks.

Energy value 255 Kcal | Protein 16.4g
Carbohydrates 26.1g | Fats 9.3g

Ingredients:

- 32.5g white flour
- 2 eggs
- 45ml skimmed milk
- 100g plain breadcrumbs
- 455g mozzarella cheese block cut into 7.5x1.25cm sticks
- Non-stick cooking spray

Instructions:

Step 1: In a shallow dish, place the flour.

Step 2: In a second shallow dish, add the eggs and milk, and beat well.

Step 3: In a third shallow dish, place the breadcrumbs.

Step 4: Coat the mozzarella sticks with flour and dip in the egg mixture. Then coat with the breadcrumbs.

Step 5: Place the mozzarella sticks onto a baking tray and freeze for about 1–2 hours.

Step 6: Grease the air fryer basket with cooking spray, then slide it inside.

Step 7: Adjust the temperature of the air fryer to 205 °C to preheat for 5 minutes.

Step 8: Press the "Start/Pause" button to start preheating.

Step 9: After preheating, place the mozzarella sticks into the preheated air fryer basket in a single layer.

Step 10: Slide the basket inside and set the timer for 12 minutes.

Step 11: Press the "Start/Pause" button to start cooking.

Step 12: After the cooking time has elapsed, remove the mozzarella sticks from the air fryer and set aside to cool slightly.

Step 13: Serve warm.

Potato Croquettes

Prep. Time
15 minutes

Cooking Time
8 minutes

Yield
4 Servings

This is a great veggie snack recipe that is packed with vibrant flavours... These potato croquettes are flavourful and nutritious. The béchamel sauce perfectly accompanies these flavourful potato croquettes.

Energy value 297 Kcal | Protein 12.1g
Carbohydrates 31.3g | Fats 14.2g

Ingredients:

- 2 medium Russet potatoes, peeled and cubed
- 15g plain flour
- 55g Parmesan cheese, grated
- 1 egg yolk
- 7g fresh chives, minced
- Pinch of ground nutmeg
- Salt and ground black pepper, as required
- 2 eggs
- 60g breadcrumbs
- 30ml vegetable oil
- Non-stick cooking spray

Instructions:

Step 1: Add the potatoes in the pan of boiling water and cook for about 15 minutes.

Step 2: Drain the potatoes well and transfer into a large bowl.

Step 3: With a potato masher, mash the potatoes and set aside to cool completely.

Step 4: In the same bowl of mashed potatoes, add in the flour, Parmesan cheese, egg yolk, chives, nutmeg, salt, and black pepper, and mix until well combined.

Step 5: Make small equal-sized balls from the mixture.

Step 6: Roll each ball into a cylinder shape.

Step 7: In a shallow dish, crack the eggs and beat well.

Step 8: In another dish, mix together the breadcrumbs and oil.

Step 9: Dip the croquettes in the egg mixture, then evenly coat with the breadcrumbs mixture.

Step 10: Grease the air fryer basket with cooking spray, then slide it inside. Adjust the temperature to 200 °C to preheat for 5 minutes and press the "Start/Pause" button to start preheating.

Step 12: After preheating, place the croquettes into the preheated air fryer basket in a single layer.

Step 13: Slide the basket inside and set the timer for 7–8 minutes. Press the "Start/Pause" button to start cooking.

Step 15: After the cooking time has elapsed, remove the croquettes from the air fryer and serve. Serve warm.

Cod Fingers

Prep. Time
15 minutes

Cooking Time
7 minutes

Yield
2 Servings

A recipe of mouthwatering cod fingers... Air frying makes a batch of cod fingers with a moist inside and crunchy outside. The wonderful coating of flour and flavour-packed egg mixture makes these cod fingers so much tastier. These crispy cod fingers go great with tartar sauce.

Energy value 483 Kcal | Protein 55.3g
Carbohydrates 38.3g | Fats 10.3g

Ingredients:

- 100g plain flour
- 4 eggs
- 2 garlic cloves, minced
- 1 green chilli, finely chopped
- 10ml light soy sauce
- Salt and ground black pepper, as required
- 3x115g skinless cod fillets, cut into rectangular pieces
- Non-stick cooking spray

Instructions:

Step 1: In a shallow bowl, add the flour.

Step 2: In another bowl, mix well the eggs, garlic, green chilli, soy sauce, salt, and black pepper.

Step 3: Coat each piece with flour, then dip into the egg mixture.

Step 4: Grease the air fryer basket with cooking spray, then slide it inside.

Step 5: Adjust the temperature to 200 °C to preheat for 5 minutes and press the "Start/Pause" button to start preheating.

Step 6: After preheating, place the cod fingers into the preheated air fryer basket.

Step 7: Slide the basket inside and set the timer for 7 minutes.

Step 8: Press the "Start/Pause" button to start cooking.

Step 9: After the cooking time has elapsed, remove the cod fingers from the air fryer and serve warm.

Bacon-Wrapped Prawns

Prep. Time
15 minutes

Cooking Time
7 minutes

Yield
6 Servings

An ultra-easy snack of bacon-wrapped prawns… These wrapped prawns are great for a snack party. Perfectly succulent bacon-wrapped prawns is one of the easiest and most delicious snacks you can make in an air fryer.

Energy value 458 Kcal | Protein 40.3g
Carbohydrates 1.1g | Fats 31.7g

Ingredients:

- 455g prawns, peeled and deveined
- 455g bacon, thinly sliced
- Non-stick cooking spray

Instructions:

Step 1: Wrap each prawn with one bacon slice.

Step 2: Place the prawns into a baking dish and refrigerate for about 20 minutes.

Step 3: Grease the air fryer basket with cooking spray, then slide it inside.

Step 4: Adjust the temperature to 200 °C to preheat for 5 minutes and press the "Start/Pause" button to start preheating.

Step 5: After preheating, place the prawns into the preheated air fryer basket.

Step 6: Slide the basket inside and set the timer for 7 minutes.

Step 7: Press the "Start/Pause" button to start cooking.

Step 8: After the cooking time has elapsed, remove the prawns from the air fryer and serve warm.

Buffalo Chicken Wings

Prep. Time
15 minutes

Cooking Time
22 minutes

Yield
4 Servings

One of the easiest and most delicious ways to prepare chicken wings… Try this recipe for Buffalo chicken wings, which are much better than those served at restaurants. These wings are sure to be a huge hit with both kids and adults alike.

Energy value 313 Kcal | Protein 44.6g
Carbohydrates 0.9g | Fats 13.6g

Ingredients:

- 910g chicken wings, cut into drumettes and flats
- 5g chicken seasoning
- 5g garlic powder
- Ground black pepper, as required
- Non-stick cooking spray
- 78g red hot sauce
- 15ml olive oil
- 30ml light soy sauce

Instructions:

Step 1: Sprinkle each chicken wing evenly with chicken seasoning, garlic powder, and black pepper.

Step 2: Grease the air fryer basket with cooking spray, then slide it inside.

Step 3: Adjust the temperature to 205 °C to preheat for 5 minutes and press the "Start/Pause" button to start preheating.

Step 4: After preheating, place the chicken wings into the preheated air fryer basket.

Step 5: Slide the basket inside and set the timer for 22 minutes.

Step 6: Press the "Start/Pause" button to start cooking.

Step 7: After 12 minutes of cooking, press the "Start/Pause" button to pause cooking.

Step 8: Flip the chicken wings and transfer into a bowl.

Step 9: Drizzle with red hot sauce, oil, and soy sauce, and toss to coat well.

Step 10: Again, place the chicken wings into the air fryer basket in a single layer and slide into the air fryer.

Step 11: Press the "Start/Pause" button to resume cooking.

Step 12: After the cooking time has elapsed, remove the chicken wings from the air fryer and serve hot.

Desserts Recipes

Hello! Please scan the QR code below to access your promised bonus of all our recipes with full colored photos & beautiful designs! It is the best we could do to keep the book as cheap as possible while providing the best value!

Also, once downloaded you can take the PDF with you digitally wherever you go- meaning you can cook these recipes wherever an Air Fryer is present!

STEP BY STEP Guide To Access-

1) Open Your Phones (Or Any Device You Want The Book On) Back Camera. The Back Camera Is The One You use as if you are taking a picture of someone.

2) Simply point your Camera at the QR code and 'tap' the QR code with your finger to focus the camera.

3) A link / pop up will appear. Simply tap that (and make sure you have internet connection) and the FREE PDF containing all of the colored images should appear.

4) If You Click On The File And It Says 'The File Is Too Big To Preview' Simply click 'Download' and it will download the full book onto your phone!

5) Now you have access to these FOREVER. Simply 'Bookmark' The tab it opened on, or download the document and take wherever you want.

6) Repeat this on any device you want it on!

Any Issues / Feedback / Troubleshooting please email: anthonypublishing123@gmail.com and our customer service team will help you! We want to make sure you have the BEST experience with our books!

Stuffed Apples

Prep. Time
15 minutes

Cooking Time
10 minutes

Yield
4 Servings

Are you in the mood to enjoy healthy apples as a dessert? This very simple recipe of stuffed apples is a must-try. This recipe requires only a few ingredients to prepare deliciously roasted apples for your dessert table.

Energy value 196 Kcal | Protein 1.2g
Carbohydrates 51.9g | Fats 0.5g

Ingredients:

• 4 small firm apples, cored
• 75g golden raisins
• 25g sugar
• Non-stick cooking spray

Instructions:

Step 1: In a food processor, add the raisins, almonds, and sugar, and pulse until chopped.

Step 2: Carefully stuff each apple with the raisin mixture.

Step 3: Grease the air fryer basket with cooking spray, then slide it inside.

Step 4: Adjust the temperature of the air fryer to 180 °C to preheat for 5 minutes and press the "Start/Pause" button to start preheating.

Step 5: After preheating, place the stuffed apples into the preheated air fryer basket.

Step 6: Slide the basket inside and set the timer for 10 minutes.

Step 7: Press the "Start/Pause" button to start cooking.

Step 8: After the cooking time has elapsed, remove the apples from the air fryer and transfer onto plates to cool slightly before serving.

Banana Split

Prep. Time
15 minutes

Cooking Time
10 minutes

Yield
8 Servings

A fruity dessert is all you need after a filling dinner... So get ready to prepare a classic fruity dessert for the whole family! Your kids will love this treat. These sweet bananas are dressed up with a delicious combo of breadcrumbs, eggs, sugar, and cinnamon.

Energy value 251 Kcal | Protein 4.1g
Carbohydrates 29.2g | Fats 10.3g

Ingredients:

• 45ml olive oil
• 120g panko breadcrumbs
• 80g cornflour
• 2 eggs
• 4 bananas, peeled and halved lengthwise
• 40g sugar
• 1.25g ground cinnamon
• 30g walnuts, chopped

Instructions:

Step 1: In a medium skillet, heat the oil over medium heat and cook the breadcrumbs for about 3–4 minutes or until golden brown and crumbled, stirring continuously.

Step 2: Transfer the breadcrumbs into a shallow bowl and set aside to cool.

Step 3: In a second bowl, place the cornflour.

Step 4: In a third bowl, whisk the eggs.

Step 5: Coat the banana slices with flour and dip into the eggs. Then coat evenly with the breadcrumbs.

Step 6: In a small bowl, mix together the sugar and cinnamon.

Step 7: Grease the air fryer basket with cooking spray, then slide it inside.

Step 8: Adjust the temperature to 140 °C to preheat for 5 minutes and press the "Start/Pause" button to start preheating.

Step 9: After preheating, place the banana slices into the preheated air fryer basket in a single layer and sprinkle with cinnamon sugar.

Step 10: Slide the basket inside and set the timer for 10 minutes.

Step 11: Press the "Start/Pause" button to start cooking.

Step 12: After the cooking time has elapsed, remove the banana slices from the air fryer and transfer the banana slices onto plates to cool slightly.

Step 13: Sprinkle with chopped walnuts and serve.

Shortbread Fingers

Prep. Time
15 minutes

Cooking Time
12 minutes

Yield
10 Servings

A traditional Scottish shortbread fingers recipe for the dessert table… This recipe prepares divinely delicious shortbread fingers with an irresistibly buttery and perfectly crumbly texture.

Energy value 224 Kcal | Protein 2.3g
Carbohydrates 22.6g | Fats 15g

Ingredients:

• 170g plain flour
• 75g caster sugar
• 170g butter

Instructions:

Step 1: In a large bowl, mix together the flour and sugar.

Step 2: Add the butter and mix until a smooth dough forms.

Step 3: Cut the dough into 10 equal-sized fingers.

Step 4: With a fork, lightly prick the fingers.

Step 5: Slide the air fryer basket inside and adjust the temperature to 180 °C to preheat for 5 minutes.

Step 6: Press the "Start/Pause" button to start preheating.

Step 7: After preheating, place a piece of foil into the preheated air fryer basket.

Step 8: Place the fingers into the air fryer basket in a single layer.

Step 9: Slide the basket inside and set the timer for 12 minutes.

Step 10: Press the "Start/Pause" button to start cooking.

Step 11: After the cooking time has elapsed, remove the shortbread fingers from the air fryer and place onto a wire rack to cool completely cool before serving.

Chocolate Soufflé

Prep. Time
10 minutes

Cooking Time
16 minutes

Yield
2 Servings

A melt-in-mouth dessert with the rich and divine flavour of chocolate… This dessert is packed with chocolate and sweetness. This chocolate soufflé is guaranteed to impress at a dinner party or a casual supper.

Energy value 603 Kcal | Protein 9.8g
Carbohydrates 54g | Fats 39.4g

Ingredients:

• 55g butter
• 85g chocolate, chopped
• 2 eggs (yolks and whites separated)
• 40g sugar
• 2.5ml vanilla extract
• 15g plain flour
• Non-stick cooking spray
• 5g icing sugar plus extra for dusting

Instructions:

Step 1: In a microwaveable bowl, place the butter and chocolate, and microwave on high heat for about 2 minutes or until melted completely, stirring after every 30 seconds.

Step 2: Remove from the microwave and stir the mixture until smooth.

Step 3: In another bowl, add the egg yolks and beat well.

Step 4: Add the sugar and vanilla extract, and beat well.

Step 5: Add the chocolate mixture and mix until well combined.

Step 6: Add the flour and mix well.

Step 7: In a clean glass bowl, add the egg whites and beat until soft peaks form.

Step 8: Fold the whisked egg whites in 3 portions into the chocolate mixture.

Step 9: Grease 2 ramekins with cooking spray, then sprinkle each with a pinch of sugar. Place the mixture evenly into the prepared ramekins, and with the back of a spoon, smooth the top surface.

Step 10: Slide the air fryer basket inside and adjust the temperature to 170 ºC to preheat for 5 minutes. Press the "Start/Pause" button to start preheating.

Step 11: After preheating, place the ramekins into the preheated air fryer basket. Slide the basket inside and set the timer for 14 minutes. Press the "Start/Pause" button to start cooking.

Step 12: After the cooking time has elapsed, remove the ramekins from the air fryer and set aside to cool slightly. Sprinkle with the icing sugar and serve warm.

Brownie Muffins

Prep. Time
15 minutes

Cooking Time
15 minutes

Yield
12 Servings

Need something wonderful to satisfy your chocolate craving? These dense and fudgy brownie muffins will do the trick nicely. This batch of decadent muffins is bursting with the taste of chocolate and crunchy walnuts. These muffins are a dream choice for chocolate lovers.

Energy value 241 Kcal | Protein 2.8g
Carbohydrates 36.9g | Fats 9.6g

Ingredients:

- Non-stick cooking spray
- 1 packet Betty Crocker fudge brownie mix
- 25g walnuts, chopped
- 90ml vegetable oil
- 1 egg
- 10ml water

Instructions:

Step 1: Grease 12 muffin moulds with cooking spray.

Step 2: In a bowl, add all the ingredients and mix well.

Step 3: Place the mixture into the prepared muffin moulds.

Step 4: Slide the air fryer basket inside and adjust the temperature to 150 °C to preheat for 5 minutes.

Step 5: Press the "Start/Pause" button to start preheating.

Step 6: After preheating, place the muffin moulds into the preheated air fryer basket.

Step 7: Slide the basket inside and set the timer for 10–15 minutes.

Step 8: Press the "Start/Pause" button to start cooking.

Step 9: After the cooking time has elapsed, remove the muffin moulds from the air fryer and place onto a wire rack to cool for about 10 minutes.

Step 10: Then invert the muffins on the wire rack to completely cool before serving.

Raspberry Cupcakes

Prep. Time
15 minutes

Cooking Time
15 minutes

Yield
10 Servings

A batch of soft, fluffy, and super-tasty raspberry cupcakes… These soft and fluffy cupcakes are filled with the deliciousness of fresh raspberries. You will enjoy a taste of summery raspberries in every bite!

Energy value 209 Kcal | Protein 2.7g
Carbohydrates 22.6g | Fats 12.5g

Ingredients:

- 125g self raising flour
- 2g baking powder
- Pinch of salt
- 15g cream cheese, softened
- 135g butter, softened
- 120g caster sugar
- 2 eggs
- 10ml fresh lemon juice
- 65g fresh raspberries

Instructions:

Step 1: In a bowl, mix together flour, baking powder, and salt.

Step 2: In another bowl, mix together the cream cheese and butter.

Step 3: Add the sugar and whisk until fluffy and light.

Step 4: Place the eggs one at a time, and whisk until just combined.

Step 5: Add the flour mixture and stir until well combined.

Step 6: Stir in the lemon juice.

Step 7: Place the mixture into silicone cups and top each with 2 raspberries.

Step 8: Slide the air fryer basket inside and adjust the temperature to 185 °C to preheat for 5 minutes.

Step 9: Press the "Start/Pause" button to start preheating.

Step 10: After preheating, place the silicone cups into the preheated air fryer basket.

Step 11: Slide the basket inside and set the timer for 15 minutes.

Step 12: Press the "Start/Pause" button to start cooking.

Step 13: After the cooking time has elapsed, remove the silicone cups from the air fryer and place onto a wire rack to cool for about 10 minutes.

Step 14: Now, invert the cupcakes on the wire rack to cool completely. Decorate with your favourite dressing and serve.

Apple Doughnuts

Prep. Time
20 minutes

Cooking Time
5 minutes

Yield
6 Servings

A sweet fruity treat, especially when delicious apples are in season… This will become a favourite autumn treat for your dessert table… These super-moist doughnuts are bursting with the flavours of fresh apples, butter, vanilla, and warm spices.

Energy value 455 Kcal | Protein 7.1g
Carbohydrates 80.8g | Fats 6.6g

Ingredients:

For Doughnuts:

- 240ml apple cider
- 340g plain flour
- 4g baking powder
- 2g baking soda
- 2.5g ground cinnamon
- 2.5g salt
- 85g brown sugar
- 30g unsalted butter, softened
- 1 egg
- ½ of pink lady apple, peeled, cored, and grated
- Non-stick cooking spray

For Topping:

- 100g white sugar
- 10g ground cinnamon
- 50g butter, melted

Instructions:

Step 1: For the doughnuts, in a large bowl, add the sugar and 35g of softened butter, and whisk until a crumbly mixture forms. Add the egg yolks and whisk until well combined. In another bowl, sift together the flour, baking powder, and salt.

Step 2: Divide the flour mixture in 3 portions. Add the first portion of the flour mixture and half of the sour cream in the bowl of sugar mixture and mix well. Add the second portion of flour mixture and remaining sour cream, and mix well. Now add the remaining portion and mix until a dough forms.

Step 3: Refrigerate the dough before rolling.

Step 4: Put the dough onto a lightly floured surface and roll into a 2-inch thickness. With a floured doughnut cutter, cut the dough. Coat both sides of each doughnut with melted butter.

Step 5: Grease the air fryer basket with cooking spray, then slide it inside. Adjust the temperature to 180 ºC to preheat for 5 minutes. Press the "Start/Pause" button to start preheating.

Step 6: After preheating, place the doughnuts into the preheated air fryer basket. Slide the basket inside and set the timer for 5 minutes. Press the "Start/Pause" button to start cooking.

Step 7: Meanwhile, in a bowl, mix together the sugar and cinnamon.

Step 8: After the cooking time has elapsed, remove the doughnuts from the air fryer and place onto a platter to cool completely.

Step 9: Sprinkle the doughnuts with cinnamon sugar and serve.

Lava Cake

Prep. Time
15 minutes

Cooking Time
12 minutes

Yield
4 Servings

A mouthwatering treat that will surely satisfy chocolate lovers… This rich and delicious chocolate lava cake is awesome. You will fall in love with this richly dense lava cake recipe with its rich molten chocolate centre!

Energy value 516 Kcal | Protein 5.2g
Carbohydrates 51.7g | Fats 32.2g

Ingredients:

- Non-stick cooking spray
- 115g chocolate chips
- 115g unsalted butter, softened
- 2 large eggs
- 2 large egg yolks
- 130g icing sugar
- 5ml vanilla extract
- 11.25g plain flour
- 15g icing sugar
- 50g fresh raspberries

Instructions:

Step 1: Grease 4 ramekins with cooking spray, then dust each with a little flour.

Step 2: In a microwaveable bowl, place the chocolate chips and butter, and microwave on high heat for about 30 seconds.

Step 3: Remove the bowl from microwave and stir the mixture well.

Step 4: Add the eggs, egg yolks, icing sugar, and vanilla extract, and whisk until well combined.

Step 5: Add the flour and gently stir to combine.

Step 6: Place the mixture evenly into the prepared ramekins.

Step 7: Slide the air fryer basket inside and adjust the temperature to 190 ºC to preheat for 5 minutes.

Step 8: Press the "Start/Pause" button to start preheating.

Step 9: After preheating, place the ramekins into the preheated air fryer basket.

Step 10: Slide the basket inside and set the timer for 10–12 minutes.

Step 11: Press the "Start/Pause" button to start cooking.

Step 12: After the cooking time has elapsed, remove the ramekins from the air fryer and place onto a wire rack for about 5 minutes.

Step 13: Carefully run a knife around the sides of each ramekin several times to loosen the cake.

Step 14: Finally, invert each cake onto a dessert plate and dust with icing sugar.

Step 15: Garnish with raspberries and serve immediately.

Chocolate Cake

Prep. Time
15 minutes

Cooking Time
25 minutes

Yield
6 Servings

What makes an exceptionally moist and dense chocolate cake? You only need to follow this easy air fryer recipe to make a perfect chocolate cake. You may be surprised at the result: a rich and decadent cake with a delicious dose of chocolate alongside cream and butter. Chocolate lovers will love this cake.

Energy value 393 Kcal | Protein 7.2g
Carbohydrates 43.8g | Fats 23.1g

Ingredients:

- Non-stick cooking spray
- 130g plain flour
- 45g cocoa powder
- 4g baking powder
- 2g baking soda
- Pinch of salt
- 130g sugar
- 3 eggs
- 120ml sour cream
- 115g butter, softened
- 10ml vanilla extract

Instructions:

Step 1: Grease a cake pan with cooking spray.

Step 2: In a large bowl, add the flour, cocoa powder, baking powder, baking soda, and salt, and mix well.

Step 3: Add the remaining ingredients, and with an electric whisker, whisk on low speed until well combined.

Step 4: Place the mixture into the greased cake pan.

Step 5: Slide the air fryer basket inside and adjust the temperature to 160 °C to preheat for 5 minutes.

Step 6: Press the "Start/Pause" button to start preheating.

Step 7: After preheating, place the cake pan into the preheated air fryer basket.

Step 8: Slide the basket inside and set the timer for 25 minutes.

Step 9: Press the "Start/Pause" button to start cooking.

Step 10: After the cooking time has elapsed, remove the cake pan from the air fryer and place onto a wire rack to cool for about 10 minutes.

Step 11: Now, invert the cake on the wire rack to completely cool before slicing.

Step 12: Cut the cake into slices of the desired size and serve.

Cherry Clafoutis

Prep. Time
15 minutes

Cooking Time
25 minutes

Yield
4 Servings

Cherry lovers, rejoice! A unique and classic French dessert of cherries for a special family feast… This classic French cherry clafoutis recipe features fresh cherries baked in a creamy vodka-flavoured custard. This delicious cherry clafoutis will satisfy your sweet tooth nicely.

Energy value 309 Kcal | Protein 3.5g
Carbohydrates 45g | Fats 10.4g

Ingredients:

- Non-stick cooking spray
- 330g fresh cherries, pitted
- 45ml vodka
- 35g plain flour
- 25g sugar
- Pinch of salt
- 120ml sour cream
- 1 egg
- 15g butter, softened
- 35g icing sugar

Instructions:

Step 1: Grease a cake pan with cooking spray.

Step 2: In a bowl, mix together the cherries and vodka.

Step 3: In another bowl, mix together the flour, sugar, and salt.

Step 4: Add the sour cream and egg, and mix until a smooth dough forms.

Step 5: Place the flour mixture evenly into the prepared cake pan.

Step 6: Spread the cherry mixture over the dough.

Step 7: Place butter on top in the form of dots.

Step 8: Slide the air fryer basket inside and adjust the temperature to 180 °C to preheat for 5 minutes.

Step 9: Press the "Start/Pause" button to start preheating.

Step 10: After preheating, place the cake pan into the preheated air fryer basket.

Step 11: Slide the basket inside and set the timer for 25 minutes.

Step 12: Press the "Start/Pause" button to start cooking.

Step 13: After the cooking time has elapsed, remove the cake pan from the air fryer and place onto a wire rack to cool for about 10 minutes.

Step 14: Then invert the clafoutis onto a platter and sprinkle with icing sugar. Cut the clafoutis into slices of the desired size and serve warm.

30 DAYS MEAL PLAN

Day 1:

Breakfast: Oat and Raisin Muffins
Lunch: Stuffed Pumpkin
Dinner: Herbed Cornish Game Hen

Day 2:

Breakfast: Courgette Omelette
Lunch: Beef Cheeseburgers
Dinner: Salmon with Asparagus

Day 3:

Breakfast: Potato Rosti
Lunch: Veggie Pizza
Dinner: Seasoned New York Strip Steak

Day 4:

Breakfast: Banana Bread
Lunch: Tofu with Orange Sauce
Dinner: Spiced and Herbed Skirt Steak

Day 5:

Breakfast: Chicken and Broccoli Quiche
Lunch: Courgette Salad
Dinner: BBQ Pork Ribs

Day 6:

Breakfast: Parsley and Jalapeño Soufflé
Lunch: Chickpea Falafels
Dinner: Spinach-Stuffed Chicken Breasts

Day 7:

Breakfast: French Toast
Lunch: Ratatouille
Dinner: Spicy Salmon

Day 8:

Breakfast: Sausage and Bell Pepper Casserole
Lunch: Veggie Bean Burgers
Dinner: Pesto Rack of Lamb

Day 9:

Breakfast: Bacon and Egg Cups
Lunch: Stuffed Brinjal
Dinner: Steak with Bell Peppers

Day 10:

Breakfast: Courgette Fritters
Lunch: Prawn Kebabs
Dinner: Glazed Pork Tenderloin

Day 11:

Breakfast: Apple Muffins
Lunch: Crab Cakes
Dinner: Herbed Turkey Breast

Day 12:

Breakfast: Salmon Quiche
Lunch: Tofu with Cauliflower
Dinner: Buttered Filet Mignon

Day 13:

Breakfast: Cheesy Toast with Egg and Bacon
Lunch: Buttered Scallops
Dinner: Simple Whole Chicken

Day 14:

Breakfast: Eggs in Avocado Cups
Lunch: Veggie Rice
Dinner: Glazed Halibut

Day 15:

Breakfast: Veggie Frittata
Lunch: Smoky Beef Burgers
Dinner: Glazed Pork Shoulder

Day 16:

Breakfast: Cheese and Cream Omelette
Lunch: Spicy Prawns
Dinner: Bacon-Wrapped Chicken Breasts

Day 17:

Breakfast: Savoury French Toast
Lunch: Buttered Crab Shells
Dinner: Glazed Beef Short Ribs

Day 18:

Breakfast: Sausage and Bacon Omelette
Lunch: Parmesan Veggies
Dinner: Maple Salmon

Day 19:

Breakfast: Courgette Bread
Lunch: Scallops with Capers Sauce
Dinner: Parmesan Chicken Breast

Day 20:

Breakfast: Parsley and Jalapeño Soufflé
Lunch: Chicken Kebabs
Dinner: Herbed Beef Chuck Roast

Day 21:

Breakfast: Salmon Quiche
Lunch: Potato Salad
Dinner: Garlicky Lamb Roast

Day 22:

Breakfast: Banana Muffins
Lunch: Chicken Kebabs
Dinner: Sesame Seed Tuna

Day 23:

Breakfast: Sausage and Bell Pepper Casserole
Lunch: Brussels Sprout Salad
Dinner: Almond Crusted Rack of Lamb

Day 24:

Breakfast: Courgette Fritters
Lunch: Spiced Lamb Burgers
Dinner: Glazed Chicken Drumsticks

Day 25:

Breakfast: Cheesy Toast with Egg and Bacon
Lunch: Prawn Scampi
Dinner: Parsley Pork Loin

Day 26:

Breakfast: Banana Bread
Lunch: Pork Sausage Pizza
Dinner: Ranch Tilapia

Day 27:

Breakfast: Veggie Frittata
Lunch: Parsley Lamb Meatballs
Dinner: Simple Turkey Breast

Day 28:

Breakfast: French Toast
Lunch: Crispy Chicken Burgers
Dinner: Simple Rib-Eye Steak

Day 29:

Breakfast: Banana Bread
Lunch: Oatmeal-Stuffed Bell Pepper
Dinner: Herbed Leg of Lamb

Day 30:

Breakfast: Cheese and Cream Omelette
Lunch: Spiced Lamb Burgers
Dinner: Spiced Whole Chicken

CONCLUSION

Air fryers have become increasingly popular in recent years, and it is easy to see why. They offer a quick and convenient way to cook food with little to no oil, making them a healthier alternative to deep fryers. Additionally, air fryers can be used to cook a wide variety of foods, from chicken wings to French fries. While they may not be suitable for every meal, air fryers are a great option for those who are looking for a healthy way to cook their food.

Printed in Great Britain
by Amazon

18513665R00059